DETERMINATION

DETERMINATION

A Journey From the Abyss of Despair

Keith Stephens Buff

Library of Congress Control Number:		2007906251
ISBN:	Hardcover	978-1-4257-8037-1
	Softcover	978-1-4257-8033-3

This book was printed in the United States of America.

To order additional copies of this book, contact:
Xlibris Corporation
1-888-795-4274
www.Xlibris.com
Orders@Xlibris.com
41289

I appreciate that you will make a donation by buying this book. However, if you would care to make a separate charitable contribution to Buff Charities, your help will be going to the following groups:

1 American Red Cross
2 Make-A-Wish
3 Operation Smile
4 River View Hospital NJ
5 Marine Corps Scholarship Foundation Central Jersey
6 Robert Woods Johnson Hospital NJ
7 Catholic Relief Services

Please make all extra donations to my foundation called Buff Charities. My web site address is called "Buff Charities. com".

Thank you. Your donation will benefit you and our world.

Be informed that one-half of all net proceeds will be put into the Buff Charities to be distributed to already selected organizations. Your patronage is greatly appreciated. My philosophy in life is that when the chips were down for me, everyone was very helpful and now it is my turn to help.

Acknowledgments

This story is dedicated to all the friends and families who have to deal with the enormous pressures of seeing loved ones disrupted on their life path. There is no easy solution to these difficult situations. In my case, the magnitude of support in every aspect was extremely helpful and inspiring.

There are so many people that I want to thank. Friends babysat for my three children and visited with me in the various hospitals. When they found out that my condition was not going to improve for a long time, they were nice enough to bring food to my family. So many kept me in their prayers. I am sincerely grateful for their very kind gestures.

Stafford Smith and my parents, Bill and Cynthia Buff, provided me with all the necessary tools from office space to the many copies needed to share this story. My mother devoted many hours a day to bring this book to market. She lived through the horror of my situation and sacrificed her free time to help edit my words. This has made it her story too.

I owe a deep debt of gratitude to all the doctors, hospitals, nurses, technicians, and therapists who worked so hard to support my recovery. I could not have done it without their expertise.

I thank all for their kindness and generosity. However, the moral support of my family and friends is what I appreciate most. Without them, I might not have attained my goals.

Chapter 1

I never saw it coming! In an infinitesimal tick of time, my life changed forever. I will tell you my story, and you decide whether it was for the better or the worse.

No one in my family had heard of it before. The words AVM (arteriovenous malformation) were to become part of their everyday language. Of course, as soon as other people heard what it was, everyone seemed to have a cousin, sister, or acquaintance who had suffered an AVM in one form or another. Unfortunately, most of the other victims had died.

The AVM struck my brain, in the cerebellum and brain stem—the parts responsible for balance and coordination. The malformation caused a weakness in the blood vessels. When it burst, it partially wiped out those abilities that had served me so well throughout my life.

On the fateful day of July 18, 1999, I was playing golf in the club championship at the Rumson Country Club in Rumson, New Jersey, one of the biggest events of the year at the club. On the way to the course, the thought never occurred to me that I would not go home or see my kids again for months. I was thirty-six years old, and my young children were at a very vulnerable age.

Life was good. I was on top of the world—no thought in anyone's mind that tragedy lurked just around the corner.

On the drive to the club, all I could think about was winning and how to secure a victory. The stress of the event was always very hard on me. There were so many details and intricacies I needed to remember in order to conquer the challenges of the golf course and play my best.

As the temperature soared to one hundred degrees on that sweltering summer day, my opponent and I toughed it out, drinking lots of water as we sweated our way through an eighteen-hole match, a preliminary round of the club championship. My game was smooth and strong that day—victory was my prize.

At the end of the match, we headed into the men's locker room for a welcome drink of cold water. Just then, out of nowhere, a sudden and excruciating pain struck me in the head. It felt like I had been hit with a golf ball. I became sick to my stomach and passed out; everyone thought I was having a heatstroke.

Chapter 2

In the locker room, my friend Doug insisted on calling 911. He had a feeling it was more than a heatstroke. His decision basically saved my life. The ambulance whisked me off to Riverview Hospital in Red Bank. In the emergency room, a CAT (computerized axial tomography) scan revealed a brain hemorrhage, not a heatstroke. These scans use x-rays to create a series of cross-sectional images of the brain and are especially useful in revealing the presence of a hemorrhage.

I was totally unconscious. My wife, Lisa, and good friend Rick McCoy stayed by my side. My mother had just returned from Ohio with my sister, Ginger, and her family, who were arriving for a week's visit. They were all at the country club pool house waiting for me to emerge from the golf course. Everyone was concerned about the fate of John F. Kennedy, Jr. The news announced that he had been lost in his airplane. Little did my family know that I was fighting for my life at the same moment.

When my mom arrived at the emergency room, the nurse, Pat, a former neighbor, comforted her. My mom noticed that while I lay unconscious on the stretcher, I acted as if I had apnea—I stopped breathing periodically and then took a deep breath to overcome it. As the results of the CAT scan came in, the nurse rushed me off to be intubated; I was unable to breathe properly on my own because of the bleeding in my brain.

As the horror of the situation began to evolve, Pat asked my mom if she wanted to contact the rest of the family, in other words, this was extremely serious. The police were summoned to inform my dad and brother Mark who were running a driving-school class in southern New Jersey. My brother Bill and sister, Ginger, were contacted at the country club pool, where they were waiting for me to join them.

The medical staff knew, at this point, that a brain surgeon would be needed. Dr. Bruce Rosenblum, reputed to be one of the top in the country, came in right away even though it was a Sunday. An angiogram, a procedure where a contrast dye is injected into an artery and then x-rayed to reveal the structure of the blood vessels, was performed. Doctor Rosenblum had his map of my brain.

He virtually saved my life, performing an emergency craniectomy, an operation on my head. As word spread, many friends and family gathered in the hospital waiting room, anxious for any news. Eventually, someone brought pizza and sandwiches for sustenance.

Chapter 3

My life, as I knew it, was changed forever. I was unconscious at the time, leaving my family to suffer through the horrors of not knowing whether I would live or die.

However, let me start at the beginning. I was born into a wonderful family, three boys, one girl. Since we were all one year apart in age, we were a close-knit group and enjoyed a multitude of activities together even though there was the requisite sibling rivalry.

Billy was born in 1960, Mark in 1961, I was born in 1962, and then our sister, Ginger, came along in 1963. She actually greeted the world on the day President John F. Kennedy was assassinated, November 22. With blue eyes and blond hair, we reminded my parents' friends of a small cadre of angels. As luck would have it, the boys got the curly hair and Ginger got the straight, which later in life proved to be a blessing so she didn't have to straighten it.

We grew up in the comfortably affluent community of Rumson, New Jersey, a town of approximately four thousand people. Nestled between two rivers, the Navesink and the Shrewsbury, we were only minutes from the Atlantic Ocean. This proximity to these bodies of water had a major influence on my life.

Rumson is home to many large, stately mansions. Treelined streets, manicured lawns, lush gardens, friendly people, our town was a wonderful place to grow up in. Part of the beauty of Rumson Road, which runs the length of the town and ends directly at the ocean, is that there are no telephone poles or high-tension wires in its entire length. All the wires are underground. This adds to the charm of a rural community.

In 1963, two weeks before Ginger was born, we moved from a small country home in Tinton Falls, to the house on Rumson Road that my parents had just built.

A white wooden sign, "Rumson—settled in 1665," sat by the road in our front yard. With majestic black walnut trees at the edge of the road, lush maple trees in the backyard always filled with chirping birds, and two and a half acres of grass, our home was handsome. A two-story house with a Cape Cod gray cedar-shake exterior, it had a gray and beige river-stone facade around the front door and was enhanced by attractive landscaping.

The ornamental cherry trees in our front yard produced cotton candy puffs of pink blossoms each spring. The reds and pinks of the rhododendrons and azaleas followed close on their bloom, and we had a gardener who trimmed and manicured the bushes and trees. Of course, weeding and cutting the grass became our responsibility as we got older. A small English-style garden enhanced the entrance to our back door. One of my mom's friends said that our house always looked like it was smiling.

(left to right)
Mark Ginger Keith Billy
1965

Chapter 4

Growing up, we were basically good kids. I don't remember anyone throwing a tantrum or whining and crying in public. Our parents took us everywhere; out to dinner in restaurants, on vacations, to sporting events, lots of exciting experiences. We learned to behave ourselves properly and reaped the benefits by being able to go with them all the time.

Our house had seven bedrooms. Each child had their own room with a Dutch door—one that was cut in half in the middle so the upper part could be left open while the lower part was closed. We never felt like we were ostracized to our room for any infraction since the top half of the door was always open. When we were very young, my mother had a live-in girl to help with our care.

A finished basement with a regulation-size pool table, shuffleboard, and bumper pool tables, an HO train layout with mountains, forests, and villages, and a slot car track provided hours of joyful playtime. Our friends loved coming to our home; we had such great games and attractions. It became a favorite gathering spot.

My parents opted not to send any of us away to boarding school. We stayed a close-knit family as we attended the Deane-Porter Elementary School, Forrestdale Middle School, and then Rumson-Fair Haven Regional High School. Many lifelong friendships were made throughout the years. My friends have been a great support to me through thick and thin.

The first time I ever lived away from home was to attend college. Northwood Institute in Midland, Michigan, taught me the fundamentals of automotive aftermarket—selling auto parts—a business my father owned.

My dad, Bill, had commuted to New York City for seventeen years, working in the textile trade. Tired of the daily grind of traveling to work, he bought a local business, Felix Auto Supply, in Eatontown, and later, a second store in Red Bank, New Jersey.

My mother, Cynthia, was what we now call a stay-at-home mom. She worked part time as a bookkeeper and volunteered with the Junior League, Monmouth Museum, and Garden Club. Eventually, as we matured and started out on our own, she taught marine biology through Brookdale Community College at Sandy Hook, a national recreation area, taking school groups for day trips to learn about the sea and surrounding environment.

I started working at my dad's auto parts store part time when I was fifteen and learned the business from the ground up; I swept floors, emptied garbage, stocked shelves, unloaded trucks, fed the guard dog, literally anything that had to be done. My college years taught me the intricacies of running this type of business, and eventually I was able to apply them to my father's company.

As my life progressed, everything seemed perfect. I had a loving wife, Lisa, three beautiful, smart, fun-loving children, Amanda, who was eleven; Lisa, Jr., nine; and Keith, Jr., five. My wife had been my high school sweetheart for five years before we married in 1985. We basically had grown up together and had a great relationship.

The auto parts company was thriving. My real estate holdings that I possessed as a business adjunct were growing. Through five different companies, my partners and I owned thirty local houses, at one time or another, that we had renovated and were renting out or selling. I played golf as often as possible. In other words, I had the world by the veritable tail. Then one day, everything that I worked so hard for was gone. Or was it?

Chapter 5

I had only been in a hospital four times in my life; when I was born, the time I needed stitches in my head after a slight conflict with a coffee table, the removal of my tonsils and adenoids, and a concussion when I flew off my bicycle. As I rode my bike down a hill, the brake handle fell off and was caught in the spokes. The bike stopped short—I kept going at about forty miles per hour. Some Good Samaritans saw what happened and stopped to help. I was only thirteen.

The pavement was harder than my head, and at first I couldn't remember my name or where I lived. It was only down the road, and as my mind cleared, I was able to tell them which way to go. They dropped me off at home; my mom took me to the emergency room.

Being confined to a hospital bed for two days was very frustrating. The worst part, though, was returning to school with a huge bandage on my face where it had connected with the pavement. How embarrassing!

The only other serious injuries I remember are a major bump on the back of my head and a broken collarbone. We had a trapeze in our garage. One day I wanted to see how high I could swing. I started about seventy yards away, ran at full speed, grabbed the bar, and swung up to the ceiling. I went so high that my hands got crushed on the ceiling. It hurt so much—I had to let go and fell over backward, hitting my head on the concrete floor.

Temporarily blinded, I couldn't even find the door to get into the house. I didn't tell my parents this until years later. The goose egg was evidence enough to let them know I really clobbered myself. To this day, I have a small bald spot where the hair follicles were killed by the blow.

On rainy days in high school, floor hockey took the place of outdoor sports. One day, running at full speed and reaching out for the puck, I slammed full force into one of the players. He was the fullback of the football team; he did not move an inch and probably didn't even know I hit him.

However, my shoulder knew it as it immediately dropped down, and I was in excruciating pain. The coach sent me to the nurse thinking it was just a bad bruise. The icepack she administered had a leak and ended up burning my skin. They told me to go home and relax.

The next morning, my sister had to help me get out of bed. My parents were away, so she drove me to Doctor Murphy, our orthopedic surgeon. The x-ray revealed a broken collarbone. He put my arm in a sling, gave me some pain pills, and told me not to play football.

School pictures were scheduled to be taken on the rock jetty by the ocean, in Seabright. I didn't want to miss my senior photo, so I took off the sling, climbed on the rocks, slipped, and tried to catch myself with my bad arm. The look on my face for the yearbook photograph wasn't exactly what I wanted it to be. I was in major pain, and it showed.

*   *   *

After many hours of microscopic surgery, Doctor Rosenblum told my parents and my wife that he had "good news and bad news." The good news: it was not an aneurism. The bad news: he was not sure what it was, possibly an AVM. He explained that an AVM was a malformation of veins and arteries that are sometimes weak in places and can burst. He had evacuated the pooling blood from my cerebellum and brain stem and hoped he had gotten the source of the bleed. Time would tell.

They wheeled me to a private room in the intensive care unit (ICU) where I could be monitored twenty-four hours a day. With my head swathed in a turban of bandages, tubes in my nose, my mouth, and my bladder, I must have been a horrible sight to see. At least I was still alive.

The doctor gave strict orders that the head of my bed was to be kept up at a thirty-degree angle at all times for proper drainage. Intravenous lines delivered Diprivan, a drug that would keep me in a comatose state so my brain could heal. Friends and family came and went, but my wife and mom spent every day with me, constantly checking to see if everything was OK.

The nurses were fantastic. They took my vital signs every twenty minutes, and three days into my ordeal, the AVM exploded again, only discovered by this constant monitoring. My neurological condition had deteriorated, and I was "posturing," pulling my arms in tight across my chest, a sign of brain damage.

Doctor Rosenblum was right on the spot. They immediately whisked me to the operating room. He opened up my head again, entering through the back of my neck as before, discovering that it was, in fact, an AVM, hoping once and for all to have corrected it completely this time. Years later, his nurse told me that he was actually sleeping at the hospital through most of this nightmare, to be available if needed.

Chapter 6

As children, we were taught the importance of respect—respect for others as well as ourselves. Compassion came along with respect. We always had a dog to care for. Panda, a black Labrador retriever, came with my father when he married my mother in 1958. He was a wonderful dog, and we all grew up together. When he died at age thirteen, we had one of his puppies that we also named Panda.

Taking care of an animal was an important factor in our lives, and we rescued a fledgling robin that we discovered floating in the river. We brought it home and tried to feed it by putting a blueberry in its mouth. It wouldn't eat at all. By accident, we realized that if we held the blueberry above its head, much like a mother bird would do, it opened its beak, squawked for attention, and then ate.

The bird grew up in our screened-in porch until it was able to fly. Uncaged, it was free to roam. Such a trusting creature, it would fall asleep sitting on our arm. As the fledgling started to practice flying, we took it outside and showed it how to catch ants and dig for worms. From then on, it lived in our yard.

We named it Bird. Whenever we went outside and called, it would fly to us, landing on our head. One day, Bird flew to a neighbor's house and landed on one of their kid's heads. They grabbed it. The poor creature must have been terrified. It probably decided humans were dangerous; we never saw Bird again. Hopefully, it went off to live with its own kind.

One day, we discovered a baby squirrel lying in the driveway, apparently abandoned by its mother; its eyes not yet open. We fed it baby formula out of a doll bottle, and it lived out on the porch in a box with soft cotton padding. When the squirrel was old enough to walk around, we let it live outside. It made a nest in the woodpile at first and then moved up into a tree. Without a mother to teach it, we wondered at how it knew to do this. Instinct is amazing.

In the morning, we would go out to greet the squirrel. As it woke up, yawned and stretched, uncurled its tail from around its body, it would climb down the tree and climb up our leg to sit on our shoulder. We fed it nuts. Eventually, it became aggressive, biting my mom when she didn't feed it fast enough. The time had come for this furry beast to go and live with other squirrels.

To this day, I find it very rewarding to help others in any way possible.

*   *   *

Unfortunately, as I lay unconscious in the ICU, a staph infection set in. I had developed a rash over my entire body, and they thought I was allergic to the antibiotic that was being administered. Several years later, we found out that I was allergic to the CAT-scan dye. An infectious disease specialist was called in, and he recommended another antibiotic to fight my particular infection. I was allergic to the new antibiotic, but it was the only answer. I had to suffer through it with major and constant diarrhea for six weeks.

In the mean time, Doctor Rosenblum decided to be very aggressive in fighting the infection and called in a plastic surgeon, Doctor Elkwood, who helped him operate on the incision, treating the infected area. They took muscle tissue from one side of my neck and skin from my thigh to close up the back of my neck. This procedure worked but left a large scar on my thigh.

While I lay in the coma, the feeding tube that was inserted through my nose into my stomach caused irritation and, subsequently, nose bleeds. I was still intubated, my breathing constantly monitored. As a matter of fact, everything was being monitored—my heart rate, my blood pressure—all hooked up to the nurses' station.

Periodically, the pulmonary team would arrive to suction out my lungs so I wouldn't get pneumonia. When we were very young, our father had promised us that if we did not smoke, when we reached the age of twenty-one, he would give us each $500. We all collected. This is probably one reason I was able to survive the AVM.

So many of my friends have told me that I am the only person they know who has lived through the devastating effects of a cerebral AVM.

Chapter 7

We started skiing when we were very young; I was three years old. At that age, you are so close to the ground that falling is not a big issue. I was also fearless. As our abilities improved and we got faster, our dad made us wear crash helmets. None of us ever suffered injuries, although we did delaminate a few skis.

Wintertime took us to ski in Vermont every weekend in our motor home, a converted Greyhound bus. As the slopes at Bromley became our usual destination, the lift operator would put an extension cord out the window so we could plug in for electricity. This way we would not have to run our generator for heat and light.

The clean, crisp air of Vermont, the winter sun warming our chilled faces, the sound of our skis gliding over the packed snow, squeaking as we made sharp turns, are all memories I continue to savor. I can still feel the crisp way my breath would freeze slightly at the tip of my nose on the coldest of days.

After a full day of skiing, when the lifts were closed down for the night, we would get trays from the cafeteria, walk up our favorite slope, called the Lord's Prayer, and slide down, totally out of control, screaming for joy, knowing that we would stop at the bottom. Those were happy and carefree times.

Each day, like a small pack of wolves, we would race down the hills, jumping from mogul to mogul, terrorizing anyone in our paths. How many times we rode on the lift became the criteria for a great day on the slopes.

We made medium-sized hills in the woods out of packed snow. As we flew over the jumps, we would cross and uncross our skis, do "back-scratchers" as we put our tips down and touched our backs with the other end of the skis; "daffies" as we put one ski forward and one ski back; "spread-eagles," arms and legs out to each side; "twists," knees bent, legs turned to one side, body facing downhill; and "helicopters" when we turned around 360 degrees.

Of course, it was important to have the skis headed straight down the hill as you landed. We had many wipeouts while learning, but persistence paid off in the thrill of landing a perfect trick. If the jumps were any higher, we would have tried flips!

*   *   *

Big stiff boots, almost like tall ski boots, were put on my feet to keep my Achilles tendons stretched so they wouldn't atrophy as I lay so still in the bed. Everyone called them my "moon boots."

My mom discovered that when I got restless and started to squirm around, if she exercised my feet up and down, forward and back, stretching the tendons as if I were walking, it would relax me. She watched the heart-rate monitor to know that it in fact was having a calming effect. I wasn't supposed to move or slide down in the bed, so that my head didn't go below the thirty-degree angle the doctor had prescribed. It was important that I stay still.

Chapter 8

Family treks to the slopes were always fun, but the one trip I think of with great humor is my journey to Vail, Colorado, with four of my buddies when I was twenty-seven. One guy's father knew someone who owned a condo there. He loaned it to us for a week. And what a week it was!

Out west, the snow conditions are superior to those in the east. No ice, lots of powder snow, glorious sunshine, and shorter lift lines. The huge mountains easily absorb the many skiers. The scenery is spectacular; the air seems so clean and crisp, even better than Vermont. But at a ten-thousand-foot elevation, the air is thinner. It is harder to breathe. We had to start out slowly until we got used to it.

Carefree days of flying down the slopes, kicking up powder, challenging hills we never should have attempted—even though we actually survived—made the days fly by in a frenzy of pleasant freedom. At night, good food and drink were our top priority.

One evening, as we all hung out at a local saloon, we set up shots of vodka along the bar. The idea was that each one of us would down the shots simultaneously. Little did one of my friends know that after the first shot, his were the only glasses with vodka, all the others contained water. We matched each other drink for drink. By the end of the evening, he could hardly walk or talk. We thought it was hilarious. About a week later, we told him all about it. He was a good sport and thought it was pretty funny too.

*   *   *

One day Doctor Rosenblum came into my room, and while pressing very hard on the right side of my chest, he yelled at me to raise my right hand. To everyone's amazement, my right arm went way up in the air—the same thing worked with my left arm. They were overjoyed to know that there was still "something" there beneath all the bandages. A cognitive spark was getting through.

At night an aide sat by my side, constantly monitoring everything. Some nights I was more restless than others. I was probably trying to climb up from the depths of darkness.

After a week, as the doctor slowly weaned me off the Diprivan, to the delight of everyone, I opened my baby blues. I don't remember any of my stay in the hospital. I am only being told about it just now.

Of course, as I regained consciousness, I started grabbing at all the tubes surrounding me. The nurses had to tie my hands down to the sidebars on the bed.

There was one nurse in particular that took a strong liking to me. She always tried to get assigned to my care and didn't like to tie me down. The doctors arrived to insert a feeding tube through the front of my stomach. This procedure is called a gastrostomy. It would eliminate the tube in my nose and alleviate the nose bleeds. The nurse untied my hands. Ahah! Freedom at last! It only took a second for me to rip out the breathing tube.

This earned me the nickname Jack the Ripper. My breathing seemed rather good, so the doctor decided to leave the tube out. Unfortunately, my larynx had become swollen from the irritation of the tube (and maybe the ripping out) and started to close up so I couldn't breathe.

The only solution was to do a tracheostomy—I would breathe through a tube inserted into my throat below my larynx. This meant that I couldn't talk. Probably just as well as I might have told everyone what my thoughts were on the subject.

This situation was very upsetting for my family for they did not know if I was capable of ever talking again as a result of the brain injury. While the tube was out, they thought they heard me say, "What time is it?" and then later on, "I can't breathe." But they weren't sure.

"On Top Of The World"
1976

Chapter 9

I had started skateboarding when I was eight. My first skateboard was literally a board. I took a two by four and screwed a roller skate onto it. As the sport became popular, I made sure I worked extra time around the house to earn more money to buy the best boards, wheels, and trucks. Trucks are the supports that hold the wheels and allow you to steer. It was always important to have the best equipment enhanced by the latest technology.

Lots of practice time paid off in handstands, headstands with no hands, kick flips, nose-wheelies, 360s, and 720s. I could spin on the front and the back of the board. Eventually, I did this with just one foot. Jumping over a bar waist high off the ground and landing back on the board was a very impressive trick.

Riding the top of a picnic table, I would "pop-a-wheelie" off the end—you push down on your back foot which raises the nose to keep the board level—fly through the air to the ground, and keep on going. Of course, there were many falls and scrapes, but I always got back up and tried harder. Patience and love of the sport paid off.

One day, a friend's father told me I could have a half-pipe ramp that was lying dormant in an old building a half hour drive away—the casino in Asbury Park. It used to be a skateboard park. I'm sure he thought we would never be able to move it.

But youth makes its own determinations. I gathered a few friends, persuaded my mother to bring an old boat trailer, and off we headed. Somehow, we managed to move a twelve-foot high, eighteen-foot long, wooden half-pipe to my backyard. It helped that it was cut into two pieces, so we made two trips. Was my dad surprised when he came home that night and found it set up in our driveway!

Years of practice helped me get on the Island Style Skateboard Team. This was a group of kids who skated for a team formed by Derf (Fred spelled backward), the owner of a surf and skateboard shop in Seabright. I won many local contests, and this led to an invitation to represent New Jersey in a competition in California. Even though I did not participate, it was an honor to be asked.

Skateboarding with my friends exposed us to many adventures. In the fall, we used to pile up dead leaves on the street at the bottom of a steep hill. I think we could get going about 45 mph. Landing in the leaf pile was the best way to stop—the most fun too.

One day, I was trying out new wheels on my board. To slow yourself down at the bottom of the hill, you would go back and forth across the hill. While I was doing this, one of the new wheels decided to slide. The board came to an abrupt stop, and I kept on going. The pavement was not very forgiving!

The half-pipe is shaped like an elongated letter U. I would fly into the air off the top of it, do a 180-degree turn while holding the board on my feet with my hand, and come back down onto the wall. Every now and then, I missed the ramp and landed in the driveway.

I learned very early to wear protective gear. Helmet, elbow pads, knee pads, wrist guards, and even padded shorts if I was practicing some new maneuver that might slam me onto the ground. I broke a few skateboards but never a bone.

At that time, skateboarding started to become a popular sport. They even built a skateboard park in Oakhurst, New Jersey, twenty minutes from our house. I spent countless hours there—the Paved Wave—with my friends, practicing, practicing, practicing. Sometimes I would ride my moped to get there on my own.

There were three different categories for contests: bowl riding, downhill, and freestyle. I excelled in the freestyle and brought many medals home to the Island Style team. I traveled around the state to parks in Seaside, Point Pleasant, Brick, Asbury Park, and Cherry Hill, which was a totally indoor park with many pools and a half-pipe run.

With a trampoline in our backyard available on a daily basis, I learned more coordination and balance, doing flips, layouts, and back handsprings. This also helped with my gymnastics at Alts for Somersaults in Shrewsbury. Around that time, we all took judo lessons too.

Not to be behind the times, our whole family learned to meditate. We were each given our own mantra that was not to be revealed to anyone. Even though I thought it was a waste of time and resented it, it turned out to be a big help, especially in my schoolwork. My grades improved. My concentration improved. My belief is that it even helped me zone in and focus when I needed to in sports.

*   *   *

Because my gag reflex was poor, actually nonexistent, I was unable to swallow properly, thus the necessity of the breathing and stomach tubes. With the tube inserted through my stomach wall, I was continuously hooked up to a gradually flowing mixture called Jevity. Something like Ensure, it provided all the vitamins and minerals I would need to sustain life. While I was in the hospital, I lost about forty pounds. My family didn't realize that I would be hooked up to the feeding tube for a whole year since I continued to be unable to swallow.

A neurologist, Doctor Pertchik, came by every day to test my reflexes. He kept close watch on any progress I made. As I touched my finger to my nose and followed his finger around with my eyes, he sounded encouraged. Little did he know that I was seeing double and had no way to tell him.

Since I was to spend so much time lying in bed, they gave me a very unique mattress. Inside it, air constantly moved in waves, up and down the length of the bed. This kept my circulation going and prevented bedsores. Special stockings manipulated my legs constantly to help prevent blood clots.

Doctor Rosenblum decided, once again, to get more aggressive. He ordered a Greenfield filter to be inserted through my groin into my vein, the inferior vena cava, to prevent any blood clots that might happen to form in my legs from traveling up to my lungs, heart, or brain. The filter looks like a small, open umbrella, facing the flow of blood, ready to catch any clot that might come along. It is made of titanium and will be in place for the rest of my life.

"Ride The Wild Surf"
1977

Chapter 10

Surfing was one of my wildest sports. Summer, fall, winter, and spring, I was in the ocean. Wetsuit in hand, surfboard under my arm, on my bike or moped, I would head to the beach in Seabright, fifteen minutes down the road from our house, every chance I got.

I started surfing when I was twelve. My balance and coordination made it a smooth transition to the ocean from the half-pipe. I was invited to join Island Style's Surf Team. The format for the summer was to have a contest every other weekend if there were waves. We accumulated points. and the year I was fifteen, I won the award for high points for the season. Hurricane waves, when the ocean was closed to all sane people, were the best. Getting tumbled and hoping you could reach the surface and breathe again was a scary feeling.

One of the most fun maneuvers was to catch a wave and "hang ten"—you would hang all ten toes over the front of the board as you rode in front of the crest. When a wave is high and starts to curl over, to be able to ride the trough it creates, known as the tube, and is one of the sensations that make this sport so thrilling.

It is very hard to describe the feeling you get from surfing. Nothing can compare. To catch a wave—experience its surge, harness its power—makes you think you're on top of the world. It is a totally natural high. There are no other distractions—no people to harass you, no phones, no monotony of everyday life. You are one with nature.

Nature is your close friend. The sea takes care of you and entertains you. There are not many people in the world who are lucky enough to experience this rather difficult sport.

Every wave you catch is different. The ocean can bring peace, happiness, and memories. There are no other words for me to describe my love of the great sea. One doesn't really know what the feeling is like until you actually experience it for yourself.

Just recently, I saw the movie *Step into Liquid*. It is a fabulous movie, depicting exciting surfing situations from around the world. The waves are majestic. The stories of the surfers who conquer them are thrilling. But the one that impressed me most was the tale of Jesse, a young man who broke his neck while surfing.

Paralyzed, confined to a wheel chair, he still went to the beach with his buddies. They would carry him to the water; he would lie on his belly on the surfboard, paddle out, and catch a wave, riding it in on his stomach. I'm sure the incredible feeling of freedom he got from riding the waves drove him to come back again and again. What an inspiration this guy is to me. He didn't give up in the face of adversity. I will never give up either.

In high school, we had a modular system for our classes. If we planned our free mods carefully, we got several hours off during the day. Although we were not supposed to leave the school premises, we managed to escape to the beach as often as possible.

A good friend of mine, Mike, would hold onto my shoulder as I rode the moped and towed him on his bicycle. We kept our surfboards at the beach club. No one was the wiser as we returned to school with wet hair, or so we thought. We hoped they would think we just got out of the shower in gym. Somehow, they must have thought we had gym every day of the week.

In the winter, the water was so cold (about thirty-four degrees) that we would get what we called "ice cream headaches" going through the waves when we were paddling out. Of course, there were no lifeguards or people around, so we took responsibility for our own lives. At the time, however, I really didn't think about it. Now that I look back, it does concern me that I took this risk.

*   *   *

While I had been clinging to life in a drug-induced coma, my family and friends kept a constant vigil. My mom arrived at 6:00 a.m. every day and stayed until midnight. My wife took some time to be with our kids but lined up babysitters and came to the hospital most of the time. Our friends were so unbelievably phenomenal, taking the children to swimming, entertaining them, and providing dinners. We never realized how much support one community could provide.

Lesley, the wife of a really good friend, set up a graph for volunteers to sign up and pick a date when they could provide dinner for my children. Others brought snacks and food to the hospital. Cards and notes came pouring in. The concern and support was overwhelming.

As an adjunct to running the auto supply business, I had worked with a real estate company over the years. Selling commercial property became a part-time job. I also worked with some partners to buy small, run-down houses, fix them up, and sell them. The workmen we used for these jobs all came to the hospital to visit. My mom would find them crying by my bedside. She ended up consoling them, telling them that I would come out of it, not really knowing if that was true.

One day, Doctor Rosenblum approached my mom. He said, "Who is this guy, Keith Buff? Everywhere I go, out to dinner or to a store, somebody runs up to me and tells me I better be taking good care of him!" I guess he thought he should do everything in his power to keep me alive or he would be in real trouble. Lots of friends were concerned with my welfare.

Chapter 11

The other water sport I loved was sailing. To be able to catch the wind, have it carry you along in its arms, silently, with just the sound of water lapping on the side of the boat was one of my best summer experiences. The excitement of competing and winning races helped me learn sportsmanship too.

Sailing teaches you more than just how to handle a boat. I learned to sail in a Turnabout, a small tublike vessel with a main sail and a tiny spinnaker that didn't look much bigger than a handkerchief. We would take another kid along as crew, but ultimately, the skipper sailed the boat and was responsible for all the decisions.

Out on the river, you know that every move is up to you—you are not relying on anyone else. Every decision—"Do I tack, do I jibe, do I go for the mark now?"—is made on your own. If you make a mistake, you try to do better the next time. If you turn over into the water, you right the boat and continue on and never give up. Even if your boat is full of water, you bail it out and keep going. These were some of the great lessons I would learn to take with me throughout my life.

Several years into my recovery, I sailed in a race with my nephew Will. I was his crew. We were in first place at the start when we tipped over into the water. The entire fleet passed us by as we struggled to right the boat. Knowing that we were in last place, we continued to race anyhow.

The satisfaction of not giving up was reward enough. We didn't need a trophy.

* * *

After three weeks in intensive care, the doctor removed the turban from my head and moved me to a room in another ICU section. All this time, my children had not been allowed to visit. They were told that I was in intensive care, and no one under eighteen was allowed. My wife really did not want them to see me all hooked up to tubes with my head in bandages. It was not a pretty sight.

One of my parents' friends was babysitting one evening. Amanda came to her after looking up "stroke" on the Internet. She was so upset and asked if her dad was going to die. She was assured that I was doing all right, and she would be able to visit me soon. What a scary time it must have been for my kids, not really knowing what was happening. Would they ever get to see their dad again?

Therapy—physical, occupational, and speech—became my entire life. While I remained in Riverview Hospital for six weeks, a therapist came every day to work with my arms and legs. I couldn't sit or stand at that point. When they finally moved me out of the intensive care unit, my children were allowed to visit.

Since I had a serious infection, all who entered my room were obligated to don a surgical mask, latex gloves, and a hospital gown. My family couldn't figure out whether this was required to protect them from me and my germs or isolate me from them and their germs.

My son balked at putting on the protective paraphernalia, but my mom told him he would look just like the doctor. He loved it and ran right in my room and gave me a big hug.

Tears of joy streamed down everyone's face. My kids were finally with their dad once more.

When my buddies came to visit, they would draw smiley mouths on their masks to make me laugh. They were a great support to me. Even though I don't remember anything about that time, I do know that they were there from the pictures my mom took.

It seems that a group would gather each evening in the waiting room. Someone would bring drinks; someone else would provide hors d'oeuvres or pizza. They had a grand old time. Actually, they were trying to make the most of a horrible situation while I sat in my room "enjoying" a slow drip of Jevity.

After the turban of bandages was removed from my head, a haircut made all my hair the same length, since it had been partially shaved. My friends thought I looked pretty decent.

Since I couldn't talk because of the tracheotomy, I had a Magna Doodle, something like an Etch A Sketch. The very first word I wrote was "eat." My family was thrilled! Not only was I hungry, they realized that I could remember the word and still knew how to write.

At the time, I was seeing double, but could not get this across to anyone. They didn't understand what I meant when I pointed to someone and held up two fingers. They thought I needed to go and do number two. I would shake my head no, and they could never figure out what I wanted to say.

I started learning how to sit up again. Gradually, the physical therapists had me get out of bed and attempt to walk a few steps. They held on to me, and I used a walker. A few baby steps across the room each day gave promise that I might actually walk again.

One afternoon (I was probably bored), I ripped out the tracheotomy tube again, further confirming my reputation as Jack the Ripper. This time, they left it out, and I was able to breathe fairly well on my own. The swelling in my larynx had subsided.

Since I needed constant doses of antibiotics, the doctors inserted a PIC line right into my vein. It would stay there for several months to make the administration of the medications more efficient.

Chapter 12

Waterskiing, wakeboarding, skim boarding, and jet skiing were great substitutes when there were no waves for surfing. As a child, I had participated on the swim team for the Seabright Beach Club. Individual races and team events brought many ribbons and medals. I was learning how to compete. Being a good swimmer helped me enjoy all the other water sports throughout my life.

My parents joined the beach club when I was three. I learned to swim in the baby pool. It was so shallow at one end that you could walk your hands along the bottom, kick your feet, and really give the impression that you were swimming. The big pool was filled with saltwater pumped from the ocean. The added buoyancy gave me an advantage with my swimming lessons. Butterfly became my favorite stroke.

On a steaming summer day, the best way to cool off was an invigorating dive off the board into fourteen feet of icy seawater. A slide provided many hours of fun too. With lots of practice and many belly flops, I perfected a triple flip off the low board. It had an adjustment for flexibility, and I would crank it to its maximum flex in order to be able to jump that high.

When I was seven, Billy, a son of one of my mom's friends, fell into the deep end of the little pool. He was only two, the water was over his head, and the guard wasn't paying attention. I jumped in and rescued him. I felt like a real hero. He is married today and expecting his own child. Perhaps, my purpose in life is to help other people in any way that I can. As a matter of fact, this is one reason I am writing this story.

*   *   *

After six weeks, I was transported by ambulance to Kessler Institute for Rehabilitation in South Orange, New Jersey, a one-hour drive from home. My wife was allowed to go with me, and Mom followed in the car. She said I waved out the back window at her, but I don't remember anything at all. As a matter of fact, I don't remember much about Kessler except hearing an announcement all the time: "Doctor exit, elevator."

It turned out that some patients were ambulatory. They wore a bracelet that would set off an alarm if they attempted to get into the elevator to "escape," thus, the announcement. Until we realized the significance of the warnings, we just thought that Doctor Exit was a very busy man.

The first night I stayed at Kessler, I was grabbing at one of the few remaining tubes in my body, the catheter. They put big, fat mittens on my hands so I couldn't grab anything. My mom and wife went home worrying about how I would survive my first night in a new location.

The next day, they removed the catheter. When they handed me a pee bottle to use in bed, I didn't know what to do with it. I handed it to my wife. She said that she couldn't use it. So I held it up to my eye like a telescope. My mom laughed so hard that she wet her pants. I still had my sense of humor.

The next day, when my family came to visit, I was sitting in a wheelchair by the elevator, waiting to go to physical therapy. They walked right by me, never expecting to see me sitting on my own. Actually, the nurse had put me in a Posey vest, a contraption that went around your chest and tied you to the chair so you didn't fall over. I had to wear one for about a week until I started sitting up on my own.

"Our Home Away From Home"

Chapter 13

While lying in bed, I thought about my life growing up. Since we were a family of six, including our parents, it would have been difficult to travel all cramped together in a station wagon. A motor home was the answer. A ski lodge, a beach house, it could accommodate us in comfort no matter where we ventured.

Our motor home, a forty-foot long converted Greyhound bus, turned out to be the best vacation home anyone could ever wish for. Every Christmas and Easter we would pack up and drive overnight to Florida. This always included a fantasy stop at Disney World in Orlando. Our destination for two weeks was Jensen Beach, on the Indian River, where we stayed on our lot at Nettles Island. What a fabulous spot! As kids, we had the freedom to come and go as we pleased, out in the boat, to the beach, to the swimming pool.

Of course, when we first arrived, our jobs were to clean up the motor home. Billy, Mark, and I were in charge of washing the entire outside, including the roof. Ginger was in charge of the wheels. Then we waxed it.

It was a lot of work, but it sure made it look nice. It was something to be proud of even though we might not have admitted it at the time. As soon as our tasks were done, we were out of there! The minibikes, bicycles, skateboards, anything that moved took us off to meet our friends that we had made over the years.

Nettles Island, a unique recreational vehicle resort, offered an incredible variety of entertainment and sports.

We played tennis, shuffleboard, minigolf; we swam in the river and the pools. Although the waves in Florida were not as big as New Jersey, we surfed and rode boogie boards as often as possible. It was nice not to have to wear a wetsuit to keep warm.

One day, a guy ran down the beach, yelling at me, "Get out of the water!" When I got up on the beach and looked back, two large fins went cruising by. Those sharks must have been at least six feet long. That stranger probably saved my life. I did go back in after the sharks were gone.

We were always doing tricks on our skateboards, setting up jumps, going down steps, wishing they would empty the pool so we could ride in it. Water skiing and wake surfing behind our whaler, skim boarding at the beach, and fishing off our dock kept us busy and happy and out of trouble. Speaking of trouble, the worst things we ever did were throw the pool furniture in the pool one night and put dish detergent in the fountain at the front gate so it blew lots of bubbles.

Pool tournaments were held periodically at the recreation center. One year, I was winning my match, and my brother Mark had lost his. I got tired of playing, so I asked Mark to fill in for me. One of the players asked me, "Weren't you the guy playing?"

I said, "No, my brother Mark has been playing the whole time, I've only been watching. I'm not very good at that game". Nobody else noticed the difference. We looked a lot alike. Mark went on to win the whole tournament!

We became members of the Family Motor Coach Association, a nationwide group of "motor-homers." The group would gather each year at a national rally in a different part of the country. We traveled to Michigan, Colorado, Oregon, and Florida with the national contingent.

The conventions usually lasted three days. All kinds of manufacturers set up their displays. There were lots of goodies to see and buy. The entertainment ranged from stage shows to tractor pulls, car races to cooking demonstrations. There was always something going on. Of course, getting to the site of the convention took us through different regions of our magnificent country, a good excuse to see some more of what the United States had to offer.

Our local chapter, the 20th Century Wagontrainers, held smaller gatherings closer to home. We always had a great time, getting together with old friends and meeting new ones. There were interesting activities for the kids, all kinds of singing and dancing, entertainment, ice cream socials, and just lots of good, clean fun in a family atmosphere.

This way of life taught us a lot about getting along with other people as they were always happy to see us. We felt very welcome and enjoyed getting together once again. Everyone pitched in to make the gatherings fun for all ages.

The activities included three-legged races, tug o' wars, egg throwing contests, to see who could keep their egg flying the farthest without cracking, water balloon fights, and talent contests, to name a few. Cookouts and potluck suppers were the usual fare. Each night we collapsed into our bunks, tired and happy, looking forward to what the next day would bring.

*   *   *

The therapy at Kessler was intense with sessions two times a day, every day except Sunday. At first, I could not sit or stand on my own, but after six weeks was able to sit up without falling over. Confined to a wheelchair, unable to swallow, I also drooled a lot. The walker was so tall that it reached my chest. I was able to lean on it and move one foot and then the other, somewhat resembling walking. At least it was considered moving around.

I rode a stationery bike. It would have been good to have a movie of some trees and fields so I would have felt like it was a ride through the beautiful countryside. Actually, it felt good just to be active again.

In speech therapy, they tried to get me to control the pitch of my voice. A Visi-Pitch machine let me see how my voice was fluctuating. The therapist would first speak into the machine so I could see how her voice flowed, and then I would try to duplicate it with my own. It was impossible for me to do at the time. The machine at least showed me what I needed to work on.

In occupational therapy, I worked with small blocks, trying to duplicate a certain pattern. This helped with my fine motor skills and hand-eye coordination. I remembered how I used to be a great pool player. Growing up, we had a regulation-size pool table, a bumper pool table, and a shuffleboard table in our basement playroom. My favorite game was eight-ball. I practiced as often as possible and could beat my opponents most every time. Now I was struggling to put little blocks together. This was a low blow.

When my kids came to visit, we would all go to the TV room. They could play some games there. We would toss a balloon around, and I practiced some hand-eye coordination as I tried to catch it. I think this gave my kids a sense of being able to help with my therapy. I can't imagine how devastating this was for them to see me in this condition. I even tried a little air hockey with Keith, Jr. He was so happy to be able to beat me.

Upon examination, Doctor Vicci, an eye doctor, discovered that I was, in fact, seeing double. He set up a pair of glasses with a prism over one eye. This helped draw the vision in my eyes together. Another doctor tried acupuncture to help with my swallowing. The results were minimal at the least.

Periodically, my friends drove the one-hour trip up the Garden State Parkway to visit. We would reminisce about the old days. Some of the employees from Felix Auto Supply came to harass me too. My wife and mom came every day. At this point, we had hired a girl, an au pair from France, to help take care of the children.

One day, a group of therapy dogs came to visit the hospital. I was not interested in seeing them, until the first one poked his head in my door. My mom said that my face lit up as the animal came in to greet me. I loved petting it and feeling its soft fur against my hands. Five different dogs came to visit that day, but the final one was a little shih tzu. He curled up on my bed next to me and proceeded to fall asleep. His handler told us that he had hair, not fur. Allergies would not be a problem. I decided on the spot that if I ever owned a dog, it would be a shih tzu.

Chapter 14

Our journey across the United States was the best trip we ever took in our motor home, nicknamed Outa Site. We were ages twelve through fifteen and wanted to stay home with our friends. But our parents insisted that it would be a great trip, the chance of a lifetime. Along the way, we all had jobs to do. Billy was in charge of calculating the gas mileage, Mark was charged with checking the oil, I had to check the air in the tires, and Ginger wrote a diary of our travels.

Dad had bought our motor home as an empty shell. Custom Coach in Columbus, Ohio, converted the forty-foot long Greyhound bus into a cozy and convenient living quarters that could sleep ten. The front door opened onto a double-size passenger seat for the navigator. The driver had a comfortable, form-fitting chair with air shocks, gentle on the back for long journeys.

It had an automatic transmission and a Detroit Diesel motor. We carried our own water supply, Kohler electric generator, and a waste holding tank. In other words, we were entirely self-contained. This was a huge asset as we didn't have to find a campground, but could stay overnight wherever our path might lead: beside a mountain lake, at the edge of the sea, next to a wildflower-filled meadow.

Moving toward the back of the bus, there were four upholstered club chairs, two on each side with a small table in between. A couch on one side and the dinette on the other, both converted into double beds at night.

Next came the kitchen with sink, stove, and oven with a refrigerator opposite. Going farther back, the bathroom included a shower. A bank of drawers and closets filled the wall across the aisle.

In the very back, two couches with two bunks that pulled down from the ceiling, cabinets, a television, and lots of drawers made a great place for us kids to spend the night. Mom and Dad slept up front. A built-in stereo system filled our home-on-wheels with music. In those days, we used eight-track tapes, the state of the art at the time.

What a fabulous trip it turned out to be! The drive west on Route 80 proved to be boring, and we griped and moaned until we got to the Dakotas. The Badlands of South Dakota were something we had never seen before. Majestic cliffs, carved by the wind, rose from the ground in an array of bright colors.

But the best part proved to be the fact that the roads in North Dakota were arrow straight, there was no traffic on them, and our dad let us drive the motor home! I felt like the king of the highway! Being only thirteen years old, this was a lot better than driving the tractor to cut the lawn.

The highway through the Badlands winds for twenty-eight miles around steep-walled canyons and fantastically carved pyramids and spires. It was a fabulous start to our journey. As we camped at the Triple R Ranch, I rode a horse by myself for the first time. I kicked him as hard as I could, but he still wouldn't run. Anyhow, the feeling of power as I sat astride the beast was gratifying.

The carved president heads at Mount Rushmore were totally awesome. Herds of buffalo dotted the fields, and every now and then we had to stop to allow them to cross the highway. It was great to get that close to such a huge animal in the wild.

Traveling through Cody, Wyoming, we stopped at the Buffalo Bill Historical Center, a museum of the old West. Indian artifacts: intricate beaded work, guns, bows and arrows, and fossils grabbed our attention.

As we waited to board the raft for our trip on the Shoshone River in Cody, my mom hugged a man and his family who were waiting to get on. It turned out to be her cousin whom she hadn't seen in twenty years. What an incredible coincidence to get to ride the rapids with a group of relatives we had never met.

Since we had never done this before, the rapids were unbelievably exciting—I remember the feeling today. As the raft bumped down the ever-changing riverbed, some areas were frothing with waves of turbulence just waiting to flip us over—or so we thought. The tour guide knew exactly what he was doing. He told us when to paddle, when to stop, and how to maneuver to navigate us safely through the rapids. The whole experience was exhilarating. Someday I plan to do it again.

The burbling and bubbling of the hot springs in Yellowstone National Park, the odd smell of sulfur, and the powerful geyser of water that erupted right on time from Old Faithful are things I will never forget. We parked right next to one of the hot springs and took an egg, put it in the water for three minutes, and it was hard-boiled! So I ate it.

At a stop in Butte, Montana, a parade was in the offing. On one of the floats, there stood, in all its splendor, the motorcycle that Evel Knievel had used when he attempted to jump the Snake River Canyon. It looked more like a rocket with some motorcycle wheels on it. As a teenager, I was very impressed and excited to come across this incredible piece of machinery.

*   *   *

One day at Kessler, someone offered me a drink of orange juice, not knowing that I could not swallow. Of course, I tried to drink it and immediately inhaled it into my lungs. My swallowing reflex absolutely did not work.

Over the past several months, I had gone through three separate sets of barium swallow tests. As I drank different liquid consistencies, from thick to thin, the x-ray machine would show the technician if I was swallowing properly. Even though the last test felt normal to me, it must have been too soon to eat as the food was still slipping into my lungs. The test showed at the time that everything was all right. This proved to be wrong.

Gradually, they began to give me some soft foods, like yogurt, applesauce, and soup. However, I still really couldn't swallow correctly. I was in pure heaven as friends brought me deli sandwiches and potato chips, sodas, and cookies. Because of this, in one week, after I thought I was having a taste of the good life again, I developed ingestive pneumonia.

At this point the doctors had sent me home saying they could do no more for me in the way of physical therapy. At two o'clock one morning, I woke up, unable to breathe. My doctor met me at the emergency room where he x-rayed my lungs to find liquid in them.

So it was back to Riverview Hospital. I stayed in their rehabilitation wing for another few weeks until my lungs cleared up. They continued my therapy there. The feeding tube in my stomach was hooked up to a machine that slowly dripped nutrition into my body. No more attempts at eating for the moment. I worked so hard trying to recapture the abilities that I had taken for granted all my life.

Christmas was coming. I wanted to be home with my family for the holidays. I made it. Wheelchair bound, dribble bib on my chest, feeding machine attached, I joyfully celebrated Christmas in my own home surrounded by my loved ones.

(left to right)
Ginger Cynthia Bill Keith Billy Mark
4th of July, 1975
Glacier National Park, Montana

Chapter 15

As we traveled north through Montana, rolling fields surrounded us, blue skies enveloped us, and majestic mountains loomed in the distance. It surely did deserve the name Big Sky Country. Our destination was Glacier National Park. The Going to the Sun Highway, which traverses the park, was too narrow for our motor home, so we rode in a White bus, an antique vehicle that used to be used as a limousine in the olden days. It held ten passengers. A college student drove and acted as our guide. The roof rolled back so we could look up at all the unbelievable glaciers and snow-capped mountains surrounding us. It was the first time I had ever seen mountains with snow on them in the middle of the summer. They were absolutely magnificent.

Water seeped through the rocks creating little waterfalls that splashed on the road, aptly called the Weeping Wall. It was the first of July and we encountered four feet of snow in the pass at the top of the mountain. A great snowball fight ensued!

After the tour, we rented some horses and rode around the edge of Many Glacier Lake. It was my second time on a horse without someone holding its head. The freedom I felt was grand; I acted like a real cowboy and started singing "Home on the Range."

The biggest disappointment of all became the Fourth of July. We were in a national park—no fireworks were allowed.

Heading north out of Glacier, we passed serene and majestic lakes. The reflections of the mountains in the water created spectacular vistas on Lake Louise and Moraine Lake.

As we continued up into Canada, we climbed the hill to the Athabasca Glacier in the Columbia Icefield. The hill was so steep our motor home barely made it. We rode out onto the glacier in a twelve-wheeled vehicle, a "cat." With tank treads on its wheels, it easily negotiated the massive area of blue ice. Chunks of ice flew through the air as the cat turned sharply. The cold wind bit into our faces. What a truly exciting experience to be able to ride across the immense frozen field. Its vastness left a lasting impression on my young mind.

On to the Calgary Stampede. The misery we had suffered because of no Fourth of July fireworks was soon to be alleviated. Chuck wagon races, rodeos, parades, a midway, and endless fireworks made this a happening not to be missed.

We had never seen a Chuck wagon race before. They were held in a large arena. Four teams competed at a time. When the starting horn sounded, each group had to load their equipment in their wagon, jump in, grab the reins, and urge their four-horse team into a dead run.

The four outriders leapt onto their mounts, and all raced together around the arena track. They thundered by, mud and dirt flying off their hooves. To add to the excitement, one horse even fell down. To our relief, he was all right, nothing injured but his pride. The team that safely made it around the track in the fastest time won a big trophy.

The huge midway offered rides and an incredible variety of games. We were in our glory. By the time we were done, the back of the motor home was filled with stuffed animals we had won. The Stampede lasts about ten days, every year in July. We only stayed one day. This far north in Canada, it stayed light until about ten o'clock at night. It was a great excuse not to go to bed.

Down the coast of the United States, we stopped in Seattle, Washington. Panoramic views from the top of the Space Needle, a leftover from the World's Fair, gave us an idea of the size and location of Seattle. The Chittenden Locks were filled with boats, and we watched, fascinated, as they rose in the waters to the next level.

Farther down the coast, we stopped in Salem, Oregon, where our motor home was to be on display for Custom Coach at a Family Motor Coach Convention. It was the most recent conversion they had built and they put us up in a hotel for three days so they could show their newest motor-home creation to the public.

Parnelli Jones, an Indy car and off-road racecar driver, befriended us. I was lucky enough to get a ride with him in his racing Jeep around the dirt track. He even had me sit in his open-wheel racecar and steer it as he pushed it up on the trailer. I was proud to be part of the pit crew.

Every afternoon, we took our minibikes out on the dirt track at the fair grounds, raced each other, and flew over a three-foot-high jump to see who could go the farthest. Mark was always the craziest, so he would win the distance award. Prizes were a candy bar or a can of soda that we had bought before the challenge.

About a half a mile away from the fair grounds, we discovered an indoor skateboard park. We walked there and had a blast. All the ramps were made of wood; that is what they used in those days. Today, most ramps are fiberglass.

When the convention ended, we continued our journey visiting San Francisco and the Golden Gate Bridge. The cable car rides were awesome, and eating at Fisherman's Wharf was a must. Many street corners provided a venue for the mimes and street musicians to perform for our enjoyment.

*   *   *

During the first winter of my recovery, I went to outpatient therapy at John F. Kennedy Medical Center in Edison, New Jersey. We ventured there three times a week, a forty-minute drive from home. Either my wife or my mom drove. Doctor Escaldi, my new doctor, set up a program, adjusted my medications, and hoped for the best. It was up to me to make it all work.

Still wheelchair bound, I was encouraged to use the walker. They had an interesting machine that helped me practice walking. With a harness hooked to my torso to hold me up, I would walk on a treadmill, trying to relearn how to put one foot in front of the other. The frustration of not being able to do what I knew I should do was not entirely devastating. I realized that as I continued to try, it was helping me.

The therapists also worked on my swallowing ability. I started eating things like bagels with cream cheese, but thin liquids continued to present a problem. We had to thicken the liquids with a special powder. It made everything taste terrible.

I met all kinds of people who were in the same boat. One of them, Walter, got into trouble one day. When his wife came to pick him up, the therapist told her that he had locked himself in the bathroom for an hour. Boy, was she furious. She yelled at him all the way out to the car. She emphasized that it was unfair to waste her time bringing him there if he was unwilling to work at improvement.

In order to get to the therapy room at JFK, we had to go down a long hallway. I started using my legs to pull myself along in the wheelchair so no one had to push me. It gave me the feeling of finally being in control of my motion, something that would help me walk on my own eventually. Having nobody obligated to push me was a great achievement.

One of the most important things I learned was how to dress myself. At home, this took about an hour. My wife would spread out my clothes on the bed. At first, she had to dress me completely. I couldn't button my shirt or tie my shoes; it took fifteen minutes to pull on a sock. Getting dressed was a major event. I thought of the days when I could take a shower and be dressed and ready to go out the door in ten minutes. Would they ever return?

Other therapies included reading, writing, fine motor skills, and speech. These would prepare me for the return to my previous lifestyle. Just picking up a coin was a challenge. I had never realized how important small achievements were. I had lost the ability to do so many little tasks that were a part of everyday living.

Dealing a deck of cards, screwing a nut onto a bolt, things that took any amount of dexterity—all became new goals to attain. Feelings of frustration, although heartbreaking, became a driving force that made me want to work even harder.

Facing the challenges of therapy made me feel like a baseball player up at bat. It was all up to me to swing and hit the ball; no one could do it for me. I always respected the position of the batter; he would stand at the plate alone, knowing it was his responsibility to get results.

God has blessed me with a unique personality trait. I will do something over and over again until I am satisfied with the outcome. It worked for my sports; now it was working for my rehabilitation. This type of persistence contributed in a big way to my continuing progress.

After eight weeks of intensive therapy at JFK, they signed me off. I stayed at home and continued my therapy at Monmouth Medical Center in Long Branch, New Jersey, a ten-minute drive from home. There I practiced going up and down some stairs. At home, my bedroom had been on the second floor, but we took over my daughter Amanda's room on the ground floor to avoid the stairs.

By the time summer came, I was eating better, able to swallow most foods without choking. The doctor removed the feeding tube. What a relief! I had been hooked up to the feeding machine every night so it could slowly drip, giving me the nourishment I needed. I had to sleep on my back the whole time. Being able to turn over in bed brought a new kind of joy.

Chapter 16

In California, traveling down narrow, winding Route 1 in a forty-foot-long motor home proved to be rather scary. Sometimes our front wheels were off the road so that the back wheels could make it around the hairpin turns. Of course, the views down the steep cliffs to the waters below were worth our efforts.

The California coast is so unbelievably different than the New Jersey coast. Wild flowers and grasses decorate the high cliffs. Jagged rocks and pounding surf adorn the beaches as sea lions and otters dot the chilly waters. A visit to the Monterey Bay Aquarium acquainted us with the sea creatures—fish, jellyfish, sharks, and eels—of the West coast.

We had never seen the likes of the Hearst Castle. The swimming pool festooned with blue tiles and gold trim was my favorite sight. Of course, to have a private movie theater in your house impressed us all.

Days of playing at Knott's Berry Farm on rides like the roller coaster that went upside down, the flume ride, and the runaway train, along with a visit to Universal Studios in Los Angeles gave us a break from traveling. We had seen the movie *Jaws* and had to go on the Jaws ride at least three times. When the shark came up out of the water to attack, we screamed with feigned terror every time.

The San Diego Zoo was the best I had ever encountered. There were no cages. The animals lived in large areas that simulated an open environment. They at least looked fairly happy.

Into the desert of Nevada, as we climbed the hill toward Las Vegas, the outside temperature reached 120 degrees. The motor home stopped four times on the way as the overheating override mechanism kicked in. We had to stop and wait for a while for the engine to cool down.

Even though we were too young to go into the casinos, we enjoyed the shows. It was so hot we didn't want to go outside. The water in our tank in the motor home was too hot to drink. It was even too hot in the pool to go swimming. So we spent our days in the air-conditioned hotels, watching shows like Circus, Circus with acrobats flying over our heads while we ate our dinner.

On to Utah, we visited Bryce Canyon. The unbelievable pinnacles of multicolored earth rise out of the canyon like striated soldiers marching side by side. What an impressive sight. They went on as far as the eye could see, spires carved as wind and water eroded them through the ages.

In Zion National Park, in the shadows of the enormous mountains, we found a stream where we continued to improve our gold-panning skills. So far, on our journey, every tiny ripple of a stream we encountered had given us the opportunity to try and perfect the unique way you needed to swish the water in the special pan in order to discover any small flecks of gold.

The only thing we ever found was called fool's gold, a mineral that sparkles like the real thing. We thought we had struck it rich as we gathered our small, shining bits of ore. How upsetting it was to eventually find out it was worthless. We had a great time collecting it anyhow.

Friends of my parents Pat and Betty Considine met us in Zion with their motor home—another converted Greyhound bus. We had been with them in Oregon, and we decided to meet and travel home together. They lived in New York.

Through Loveland Pass in Colorado, we drove by the ski resorts of Vail and Aspen. The thin air of the ten-thousand-foot elevation made us all feel a little dizzy, but the views of the mountains, some with small patches of snow still clinging, were spectacular. I hoped someday to be able to return there to ski.

On our way home, after our six-week-long adventure, Pat and Betty insisted that we stop to visit some friends of theirs in Brookfield, Ohio. We finally agreed, after much prodding, that we would stop for no more than three hours. Three days later, we finally left. It turned out that the Kirila family, three boys and a girl, just like our family, lived on an estate with a man-made lake in their backyard. Gene, the father, was in the construction business and just dug a humongous hole in their yard and filled it with water.

We water-skied until we couldn't walk anymore. Then we rode horses, minibikes, four-wheelers, bicycles, and skateboards. We swam in the lake and their indoor pool. When our parents finally dragged us away, we were definitely waterlogged. As it turned out, my sister was twelve, and Gene, Jr., the oldest of the Kirila kids, was also twelve. They didn't know at the time that they would eventually marry each other and have four children of their own.

*   *   *

A friend of my parents sent them an article about the use of hyperbaric oxygen therapy for brain injuries. After researching it on the Internet, my mom found the name of a doctor in New York City, Doctor Calapai. In the middle of July, in the heat of the summer, we trundled off to the city.

Parking is a big problem in NY. There was a hotel around the block from the doctor's office. My mom paid the doorman to let us leave the car out front for a couple of hours. He would always help get me out of the car and into the wheelchair, a really nice guy.

The theory behind hyperbaric oxygen therapy is the introduction of pure oxygen under pressure so that it saturates the damaged tissues of the brain where oxygen no longer reaches. It is used in hospitals to treat sores that will not heal. This is especially important for people with diabetes. Because, at the moment, it has not been FDA approved for treating brain trauma, hospitals cannot participate.

The machine in Doctor Calapai's office consisted of a stainless steel cylinder that would accommodate one person. You had to lie down on a wheeled table as they pushed you into the cylinder. The top had a glass area so you could see out. Then they closed the door and sealed it. I could communicate with the technician through a speaker.

In order to prevent any sparks, I had to don an all cotton hospital shirt and pants. The treatment lasted one hour. I was taken to a pressure of one-and-a-half atmospheres. At sea level, one atmospheric pressure is approximately fifteen pounds per square inch on your body. With the added pressure in the machine, pure oxygen was being forced into my damaged brain cells.

When they finally opened the door and wheeled me out, I was soaked in perspiration from head to toe. The inside of the cylinder is air-conditioned. The temperature had been very comfortable. Why had I been saturated with sweat? How had this happened? The answer came during the next visit.

I went for treatments twice a week. The second time, I was in there for about ten minutes when I gave the finger across the throat signal to the technician—"Get me out of here!" He immediately dropped the pressure and opened the door. I was having an anxiety attack. I was claustrophobic. I couldn't stand another second of it.

From then on, I had to take Valium about an hour before my treatment in order to tolerate the enclosed space. It probably was the reason I had perspired so much the first time—I had been anxious but didn't even realize it; that's how out of it I was at that stage of my recovery.

One week, my mom made arrangements for me and my wife to stay at the hotel around the corner. We had a great dinner at the Palm Restaurant and then went to see the Broadway show *The Lion King*. It was fabulous. What a treat to finally be entertained!

A series of ten treatments seemed to have brought results as I finally decided to get out of the wheelchair. Up until this point, I had felt that this was all just a bad dream. The treatments helped me become more aware of what was really going on. I started regular physical therapy with a great guy named Joe McAuliffe.

It took many months to even get an appointment with him; he was so booked up. He ran his own physical therapy business and had worked with his father, helping him overcome his disability as the result of a massive stroke. Joe knew what to do to help resurrect my balance and coordination. As soon as I started there, he said, "Boy, you will get out of that chair!" And I did.

Chapter 17

Mobility was always an important factor in my early life. We carried two 50cc mini Honda motorcycles in the storage compartment under our motor home. Whenever we had a chance, we hopped on them and flew around our yard or whatever parking lot was convenient. From eight years old onward, I rode some form of motorized vehicle. By the time I was thirteen, my moped made me very independent as I went to school, then off to any sport that took my fancy.

Everyone in our family had to take turns cutting the two acres of grass in our yard. The ride-on mower taught us driving skills we would use forever. Later on, I took advantage of this experience as I raced my car in gymkhanas and time trials.

Much of my automotive knowledge came from rebuilding my first car, a Volkswagen Beetle. I bought it used; there were megamiles on it. I was lucky enough that my dad was a car nut and had all the tools necessary to work on an automobile.

Although he didn't help me do the mechanics, he acted as my guide. This way, I learned how to do the work and was extremely proud of my success, especially when it actually ran. The addition of "headers" raised the decibel level of the exhaust to neighborhood-complaining volumes. It also gave me 10 percent more horsepower, an important factor in my life at the time. At that stage I was a teenager.

My next car was a Toyota Celica. By then, I was driving in time trials—events held in large parking lots where you drive through a course set up with cones, racing against the clock. The best time wins. My car was equipped with headers, a rejetted carburetor, adjustable racing shock absorbers, a three-quarter camshaft, race springs that lowered the car, and Pirelli tires. I won quite a few trophies. It was fun and enhanced my driving skills at the same time.

My dad was a semiprofessional off-road rally driver. He raced all over the country and won many events. The team consists of a driver and navigator who tells the driver when and where to turn, an extremely important role as the car is traveling at breakneck speed over the course.

The race consists of timed stages; you receive points for being at the checkpoint at the correct time, not too late and not too early. Since you do not know where the checkpoints are going to be, you must consistently stay on track and on time. Most of the courses were run on backcountry roads and in the woods.

One summer, the Wing and Bonnet Car Club held their annual off-road rally in the New Jersey Pine Barrens. I entered, driving my Celica. My brother Bill navigated. Everything was going great until we made a wrong turn, ended up on the highway, and a cop stopped us for speeding. When he saw the rally numbers on the side of the car, he had no mercy. We ended up finishing the rally at 2 am; everyone else had come in around 10 pm and thought we were lost forever in the Pine Barrens. That was the end of my rally days.

On the course, we had seen a Porsche that had failed to make its turn and plowed into the front of a house. Not a pretty sight, it at least told us where we should be making our turn. Several legs later, we ran into a ditch on the course. The car became airborne; we landed on the front tires and cracked the windshield. I hit my head on the ceiling. It was a good thing we were wearing crash helmets and safety belts.

Since my college days were spent in Midland, Michigan, I needed studded tires on my car. This proved interesting when it came to entering autocrosses. In one particular event, as the course in the parking lot was partially snow-covered, I swapped one rear-studded tire to the front so it gave me better traction front and rear. By doing this, I won the event easily, beating out twenty other competitors.

*   *   *

My new therapist, Joe, holds the world record for bench pressing 527 pounds. He is about five feet and five inches and solid muscle. One day, while he encouraged me to balance on a roller, I hit him in the chest (only in jest). He said, "Nobody hits *me*!" Everyone had a good laugh about it.

Another day, he made me laugh so hard that as I took a drink of water, the water sprayed out my nose. I would tell him jokes. When I started cracking up over the punch line, he would tell me that I was my own best audience. It did help to keep a sense of humor.

As my muscles became more active, my balance began to improve. When I first started doing lunges, I had to hold on to bars on either side of me. Eventually, with Joe's encouragement I could manage lunges all the way across the room, not holding on to anything. At first, I could only work out on the elliptical machine for about one minute. As my stamina built, I eventually managed thirty minutes.

In the beginning, I could bench press fifty pounds. After three months of working out, I pressed 150 pounds. Joe was concerned about letting me try more since I had an AVM, and there still might have been a residual weakness in my brain. He did not know how right he was. I dreamed of the day when I could press 350 pounds like I used to do after I graduated from college.

For leg strength, I stepped up and down on a one-and-a-half-foot high platform. Squats, free weights, push-ups, sit-ups, pull-ups were among the many exercises I managed to perform with Joe coaching and pushing me all the way. Work with a medicine ball helped with my hand-eye coordination. Joe became a very good friend, one of the many who helped me through this difficult time.

Chapter 18

At home in Rumson, I never got into too much trouble. However, one night, Mark and I were hiding in our bushes, throwing snowballs at cars as they passed on Rumson Road. I made up an ice ball and told Mark, "One more car and then we'll stop." The car came—I threw the ice ball.

As it was lofting through the air, I saw the car. I started praying, "No, no, pleeease don't hit it." But it was too late. Mark had yelled, "Cop!" before I threw it, but I couldn't stop the forward motion. A resounding thud told me I had found my target, probably scaring the police officer half to death.

We ran for our lives. The spotlight on the top of the squad car followed us to our backdoor. My mom asked, "What's wrong?" as we raced past her, looks of abject terror on our faces. She went to the door with a smile on her face to greet the policeman. He said, "Ma'am, this is no laughing matter."

Writing one thousand times, "I will not throw snowballs at cars," cured us of ever doing it again. Plus, understanding that it could have caused somebody to have a heart attack was not something I had even considered. It helped me learn that you are responsible for your actions and must accept the consequences.

*   *   *

Toward the end of the summer, a little over a year after my disabling injury, I was accepted at Hartwick Brain

Trauma Unit in Edison, New Jersey, on the recommendation of my doctor from JFK. At that point, I could walk on my own but needed someone or something to hold on to in order to maintain my balance. Many sessions of speech, occupational, and physical therapy continued. They threw in some mental counseling too.

The pool table in the all-purpose room kept beckoning to me. One day, I tried it. The surprise of the day came as I walked around the pool table on my own, setting up shots, actually sinking balls. From then on, I knew I could maneuver on my own, even though I fell a few times. I always got up and tried harder.

When it was time to leave Hartwick, the counselors told my wife and mom that the condition I was in was probably all that I was going to realize. There might be some progress, but probably not much more. I cannot thank my mother enough for not accepting their diagnosis. She chose to have hope, and I thank the Lord for her decision.

I think that was when my wife decided she had had enough. She would not live with a cripple the rest of her life. In retrospect, she probably should have gotten a nurse to take care of me instead of getting an au pair to take care of the children. But she wanted to be in charge of my care. I thought her love for me would stand up through all adversity. Obviously, it couldn't.

In November, my wife packed up the children and the dog and moved to her sister's. We had gotten a shih tzu puppy and called him Rusty, after the surfboard manufacturer. My wife had given me an ultimatum: we would get a dog or she would go out and get a job. I opted for the dog because I didn't think my wife should have to go out to work. After all, I had always been the provider for my family.

Chapter 19

Football was another of my favorite sports. When I was young, it was junior peewees. We basically ran back and forth on the field and sometimes caught the ball. I played offense and defense in high school and loved it.

One year, our team, the Rumson-Fair Haven Bulldogs, won the B State Conference championship. Although our team was smaller in stature than most of our opponents, we outplayed them that year with quick thinking and intelligent maneuvers encouraged by our coach.

But when I went to college early in my first year and saw the humongous size of the players, I decided it was not the sport for me. I tried it out for two weeks. That was enough. I didn't feel like dying at such a young age. The coach tried to convince me to stay so the other players would have someone smaller to boost their egos. I was smarter than that.

One of the advantages of getting ready to play football was that I realized I needed to bulk up and build up some muscles. All my life I had been small. My brothers picked on me a little; what else are siblings for?

My dad suggested I join a gym and use the weights. Boy did this work! One day I was watching a football game on TV in our playroom. Billy came in and just changed the channel without asking. I said, "Hey, I was watching that!"

He said, "Too bad." I got up and threw him over the couch. He never teased or tormented me again.

*   *   *

Financially, we were in pretty good shape. Fortunately, I had taken out a private disability insurance policy. This monthly payment, along with my social security disability, allowed me to pay the mortgage on our house and buy food and clothing.

But, as I said, my wife gave up on me. Since the children had all their belongings at our house in Little Silver, I chose to move in with my parents and let my wife and the children live in the house. She filed for divorce. This was a devastating time for me. Depression became a major concern. How was I to go on living? Everything had been taken from me at this point.

When the doctor told me that I would never walk or talk properly again, I became very upset. This also made me very angry. My life had been totally interrupted. What was I to do? It would have been so easy to give up and just remain in the wheelchair for the rest of my life, being fed through a tube. Suicide even crossed my mind. But this was not to be.

At Hartwick, they taught me to write everything down that I was planning to do for the day. I continue to carry a small notebook in my pocket, jotting down notes as they cross my mind. I have a large planner where I continue to write down my daily activities. It is so helpful not to have to remember everything at once.

My long-term memory is fantastic; however, the injury has caused some short-term memory loss. When the AVM burst and the blood entered my brain, it caused damage to that part of the brain that controls short-term memory. As I get older, I'm sure the loss is getting worse, at least according to the experiences of my parents and my friends.

They all say it's normal. I'm just a little worse than normal. But who knows what normal is?

I was also taught to weigh the pros and cons when trying to make a decision. By jotting them down on paper, I could study the options before deciding what to do and was better equipped to choose a course of action. Even if I didn't want to, I would go with the pros when they outweighed the cons.

An important decision I made in this manner was whether or not to see a doctor in New York City who worked with Botox injections, Dr. Andrew Blitzer, an internationally known otolaryngologist, one of the best in the field. The idea was that if I had Botox injections in my throat, it would help with my speech and swallowing. I did not want to go, but after studying the pros and cons, I made the informed decision to see the doctor.

My mom took me up to Saint Luke's-Roosevelt Hospital Center. After he examined my throat using a tube inserted down through my nose, he informed us that I had a myoclonis in my throat, a constant spasm of the muscles. It was the first time we heard that word. He would not give me the Botox injections because it would adversely affect my swallowing. Hopefully, medication would control the spasms.

Doctor Pertchik, my neurologist, prescribed different medications throughout the years. Many of them made me dizzy and threw me off balance. I had to stop taking them. Most of them were medications for people with seizures. I had actually never suffered a seizure throughout this whole ordeal.

My parents own a condo in Long Branch, New Jersey. When my wife abandoned me, I moved in with them. Every year, they go to Florida for the winter— to Nottles Island. So, guess where I got to go?

Chapter 20

When I was young, in order to earn more money than my allowance provided, I landed various odd jobs around the neighborhood. Along with Billy and Mark, and sometimes on my own, we washed cars, cut grass, fertilized lawns, raked leaves, picked up sticks, and shoveled snow. I also had my own paper route, delivering to my customers on my bike, through all kinds of weather. This is how I earned my skateboard, surfboard, bicycle, and moped. Eventually, I bought a car.

When I started working for my father in the auto parts business, I managed to take a company that was doing well and made it do even better. It required many hours of hard work, but the results of its success were well worth my effort. Putting in seventy-three hours a week helped accomplish my goals.

Using my imagination to see the future enabled the company to grow. The potential that a person has when they use their imagination is almost unstoppable. Having good friends to help me financially was a big asset. It was gratifying to have them all believe in my dreams to make the business the success that it became.

As I worked my way up the ladder in the company, I found myself at the front counter selling parts, not really knowing what I was doing. As I asked my employees questions, they just laughed at my ignorance. Boy, was I ever humiliated! It made it hard to give them direction when they really knew more than I did. By working side by side with them, I eventually earned their respect, and they no longer laughed at me. I had learned a lot.

This practical, hands-on experience only enhanced my college education. Running the company was enjoyable but very stressful. Trying to keep the employees, suppliers, and customers happy at all times was a major undertaking. The jokes and good times we had at the store will stay forever in my memory. Lasting friendships were made and continue today with many of my customers and business associates.

As we put together our advertising, we always used the aspects of pain and pleasure. For instance, when your car wouldn't start (pain), you could come to Felix Auto Supply to get what you needed (pleasure). We saw that with this approach the advertised sales went over very well.

It was a great asset and comfort for me to have a job made available immediately after my college graduation. Some kids today with college educations are finding it hard to get a job. I was lucky enough to never have to go for a job interview. Instead, after a few years, I was interviewing potential new employees. I realize how important a college education is for success in the workforce. However, many of my employees never went to college, and they knew more than I did.

When I was first married, we bought a small house that needed work. After fixing it up, subdividing the property, and selling the house, we were able to afford a larger home in Little Silver.

Right next to the town where I grew up, it was a prime location, friendly neighborhood, right down the street from our church and the children's school. With a large backyard that backed up to a four acre, state-owned nature preserve, we enjoyed the birds and wildlife that came to visit. A deer, raccoons, egrets, and butterflies frequented the yard to the delight of the children.

One of the most devastating experiences was the loss of the auto parts company I was running for my father. As I became disabled and unable to go to work, we mistakenly thought that the employees were capable of running the business on their own. Most of them had been with us for over ten years.

They tried their best, for which I am eternally grateful. But as some customers chose not to pay and some suppliers put us on a cash only basis, the company got deeper and deeper in debt. It became apparent that we would have to close the doors. My hope was to take over again once my recovery was complete, but since my suppliers and customers "kicked" me when I was down, this was not to be.

Even though this situation was devastating for me, the writing was on the wall. The auto parts business was changing dramatically. Most new cars are equipped with computers, so repairs are done by the dealerships. The backyard mechanic is becoming a thing of the past. Our company could not survive on the small mechanic shop business; the car dealerships and garages were buying direct from the warehouses.

Many of the new cars are bought on a lease basis, so they were being repaired only as needed. As the lease would run out, instead of reselling the car, it would be sent overseas about eighty percent of the time. Repairs were not part of the picture. I had to look at the positive side of closing the business. Perhaps its time had come.

Running a business had required hours of dealing with other people: employees, customers, suppliers, salesmen, and bankers. Happy to provide a means of income for my employees, I realized that my efforts to keep the business viable were of the utmost importance. This had put a ton of pressure on my shoulders.

In many situations, not only in life but in business, we tend to focus on all the bad things that could happen if we try something new. We neglect to hone in on the possible good results. In making many decisions, there always seemed to be some factors that would prevent me from moving forward. I would only focus on the positive outcome and try to ignore the negatives. The end result became my objective. My philosophy has always been "use it or lose it."

To this day, some of my former employees still call me for lunch dates. They are so happy to see my progress. It is good to have a continued rapport with them. When working each day I was living for the moment until the moment changed my thinking.

Financial freedom became a worry. With the income from my Social Security and disability policy, I was able to stay afloat. It had been suggested that I declare bankruptcy. This decision would not have sat well with me, so I chose not to.

During my years of managing the auto parts supply store, I also invested in real estate. With several partners, we bought small houses, renovated, and sold or rented them. Since this market proved to be lucrative, I purchased some houses for my own personal investment. I always bought the house with a resale figure in mind. The amount of renovations increased the value of the property.

In regard to my associates in the real estate investment group, the people that I thought were reliable and trustworthy turned out to be interested only in the betterment of their own lifestyles. Even though I had supported them financially, they chose to give me the short end of the stick. When I became disabled, these supposed friends were hopefully going to help me.

Their own greed proved to be more important to them than their concern for my condition. The sad part about their actions is that they all knew I would have been willing to help them if the situation had been reversed. As a result, I had to resign from the investment groups, and they subsequently closed down.

The loss of good friendships is very hard for me. I am sure they are at a loss also without my constant support in making business decisions. I am not a vengeful person, but to kick somebody when they are down is wrong.

One minute I was gliding along in life and then most of what I had built was falling apart without my guidance. To lose everything I had worked so hard for over the years was a major blow. My father had given me the opportunity to run a local business. I had built it up to be a thriving entity and had made a very comfortable living for my family. The real estate investments had flourished under my direction.

On the other hand, many of my faithful and good friends helped me get back on my feet again. For their kindness and support, there may come a time when my efforts will be there for them too.

After my wife decided to leave me, our comfortable home in Little Silver had to be sold. I was no longer in a position to maintain it. The rule of thumb is that it takes 10 percent of the value of the property to be able to meet all the expenses on an annual basis.

The house had been a dream come true. It broke my heart to have to give it up. I had put many hours of hard work into making a happy home for my family. As all my personal property and furniture was disposed of, I turned the page on my former life. It was time to move on and start a new chapter.

*   *   *

According to the National Institute of Neurological Disorders and Stroke, arteriovenous malformations (AVMs) are defects of the circulatory system. They consist of a snarled tangle of arteries and veins. An AVM can develop anywhere in the body. Mine happened to be in my cerebellum; when it burst, the bleed affected my brain stem as well. According to statistics, AVMs of the brain and spinal cord (neurological AVMs) affect approximately 300,000 Americans, with no regard to sex, race, or ethnic background.

Most people don't even know they have them. I certainly never knew that anything was amiss. As a kid, I had some headaches that would send me to my bed for a few hours until they went away. My parents took me to a doctor who x-rayed my head. Nothing seemed to be wrong.

Of course, there were no MRIs or CAT scans in those days. If so, the AVM probably would have been discovered and something could have been done about it. But who knows? Maybe the treatment would have been invasive. Maybe I never would have surfed or skateboarded or played golf. It is too difficult to try to guess what might have been. It is better to deal with what exists in the best way possible. That is what I do.

Some people with AVMs experience symptoms such as paralysis or muscle weakness. I had none of this until it ruptured. Then I was left with all kinds of symptoms. Ataxia is the name given to loss of coordination. It was a new word to my vocabulary; I was to hear it over and over again through my years of rehabilitation.

It seems that these abnormalities can gradually build up, eventually causing neurological damage, usually to people in their twenties, thirties, or forties. Sometimes, the

AVM will reduce the blood flow to the brain, resulting in oxygen depletion and damage. Others might compress or displace parts of the brain or spinal cord. As in my case, the AVM might hemorrhage into the surrounding tissues.

My hemorrhage occurred in my hindbrain. The hindbrain is formed from two major structures: the cerebellum, which is nestled under the rear portion of the cerebrum, and the brainstem, which serves as the link between the upper portions of the brain and the spinal cord. These structures control finely coordinated movements, maintain balance, and regulate some functions of internal organs, including the heart and lungs. Damage results in the loss of the ability to coordinate complex movements such as walking and talking.

The resulting lack of coordination therefore affected not only my ability to walk but my speech. It is amazing how many things one must control in order to talk. Breathing, tongue and mouth movement, pitch, and volume were all things I needed to learn and master all over again.

One of the exercises my speech therapist taught was to lie on my back on a flat surface and breathe from my stomach rather than my chest. She put a book on my stomach so I could see it going up and down. I had to do this for five minutes every day. It was very difficult at first to remember to force my breath from my abdomen in order to talk more clearly.

Speech therapy had started while I was in Kessler and continued for five years. Every hospital I went to had a speech therapy department. A therapist even came to my home for sessions. Hours and hours of working just to make myself understood have paid off. Most people understand what I am saying now. I don't have to repeat myself as often as before, although you can tell that I still have a problem.

When I lived in Florida with my parents, I went to the Cleveland Clinic in Fort Lauderdale. There the therapist started using an E-Stim machine that emitted a small electric shock, pulsing every twenty seconds. The electrodes were attached to my chin for fifteen minutes and then my throat for fifteen minutes, hoping to alleviate the myoclonis, the continuous tremor in my throat.

When I started with this treatment, I also had a tremor in my upper and lower lips and chin. These eventually went away. I bought a machine to take home and used it every day for about a year.

I do not know if the myoclonis has gone away yet as I have never been able to actually feel it. I am now taking glycogenic sugars to try and heal the connections in my brain and feel I am speaking better already. These are glyconutrients made from fruits and vegetables.

The product, called Ambrotose, supports the immune system. It enhances cell-to-cell communication. Many of my friends have commented on the increased clarity of my speech. With a long way to go, I continue to work on voice exercises at home. No more speech therapists for a while.

Throughout all my therapy and dedication to improve, one of the most important aspects of my attitude was laughter. The old cliché "Laughter is the best medicine" is so true.

At first, my mother was frustrated over my condition. I was slow. Sometimes I didn't understand what to do. She realized that patience would be of the utmost importance. With patience and understanding came laughter and joking. To this day, we laugh all the time about so many little situations. It is the best way to deal with frustration.

"Teeing Off"
Myrtle Beach, South Carolina 1989

Chapter 21

Tennis, football, soccer, baseball, racquetball, paddle tennis were all the ball sports I enjoyed, but the best of all turned out to be golf. As a boy, I played in the junior golf program at the Rumson Country Club. We started with one, advanced to two, and then three holes. I played in some Parent-Child Tournaments with my mom and dad, and we did very well. But I never took it up in earnest until I turned twenty-three. By then, I was married and running the auto parts business for my father.

I'll never forget the first time I went out to play golf with my friends. I managed to hit the ball three whole yards and was never so embarrassed in my life. Determined not to have this happen again, I took up golf with a vengeance.

Books, magazines, videotapes, and other various paraphernalia got me going. Of course, multiple lessons with golf professionals and myriad hours of practice brought me to the point where my handicap reached its lowest point—one. I even won the Rumson Country Club A-flight Championship one year, and then two years later moved up and became the club champion, which I managed to do two years in a row.

My golfing friends began to call me the Grinder because I would always wear my opponent down. I would rather be remembered as a good guy—a guy who is gritty and never gives up.

Golf became the most addictive sport I have ever played. Not only did I have a great time with my friends,

I made many good deals with my business associates on the golf course. Suppliers and customers ran golfing events and always asked me to participate. The rapport I built with them was very important for the success of the company.

When you are playing with an individual, you find out very quickly what type of person they are. It helped me decide if I wished to be involved with them in the business world.

Golf is a game that can only be played and never be won. No matter how well you do, you always say you could have done better. It is one of my favorite sports—one of the greatest games because it's only you and the ball. When you hit the ball, you can't blame anyone for a bad shot but yourself.

It is definitely a mind game. Having the right attitude can make or break your score. Of course, a little bit (or maybe a lot) of luck surely helps. Trips with my golfing buddies to many great courses such as Pine Valley, New Jersey; Winged Foot in NY; Jupiter Hills and Sawgrass in Florida; Myrtle Beach and Harbor Town, South Carolina; and Mid-Ocean in Bermuda made golf an incredibly enjoyable event.

*   *   *

The physical therapist at the Cleveland Clinic helped me tremendously. He was a golfer. Among many other exercises, he taught me how to keep my balance through a golf swing. One day, I met him at the range so we could practice. Inspired to try my favorite sport again, every now and then I actually connected with the ball using my 5-wood, and it flew about 150 yards, a far cry from the 200 yards it used to average.

I knew I couldn't hit my driver or 3-wood at this point. It was frustrating and disheartening not to be able to play the way I had in the past, and I realized at this time I had a long road ahead of me.

While in Florida, I went to the source of hyperbaric oxygen therapy. The Ocean Hyperbaric Center in Lauderdale-by-the-Sea is the office of Dr. Richard Neubauer, the pioneer of this type of treatment for brain trauma. I spent two weeks at a time there.

Twice a day I entered the tank. This time, I could sit up in it, look out through a large glass porthole, and watch videos. It made the hour in the tank go pretty fast. I didn't need to take Valium, but I did have to don the all cotton hospital outfits so there would be no chance of creating sparks from my clothing.

Again, I was taken down to one and a half atmospheric pressures, pure oxygen being forced into my damaged brain tissues. With two sessions a day for two weeks, I received twenty treatments at first and returned three months later for twenty more.

A scan before and after treatments revealed improved circulation in my brain. Hyperbaric oxygen therapy is presently used to treat near-drowning victims, stroke, cerebral palsy, coma, Lyme disease, traumatic brain injury, cerebral edema, migraine, chronic fatigue syndrome, peripheral neuropathy, multiple sclerosis, osteomyelitis, burns, gas gangrene, crush injuries, and carbon dioxide and cyanide poisoning. I do believe it was a tremendous help in my recovery.

While I was being treated in Fort Lauderdale, the doctor suggested I try a clinic in Delray Beach, where the therapist worked on balance problems. Their form of therapy consisted of spinning. While the patient sits in a chair, the therapist starts it spinning, five times to the right, then five times to the left. Each day the spin is increased by one until you reach twenty times to the right and twenty times to the left.

The theory behind it is that the inner ear, which affects balance, is put back into equilibrium. I bought an office chair that spins so I could continue this therapy at home.

One weekend, I decided to take a break and not spin at all. By Sunday, I lost my balance and fell to the ground. To this day, I spin. Does it help? Who knows? But as I said before, I will try anything. Something is helping. Is it just my determination to get better? Maybe.

While in Fort Lauderdale, we went to the beach every opportunity, in between oxygen treatments. I was only allowed to be in the chamber twice a day for one hour at a time. It is like a decompression chamber that is used to treat scuba divers who have gotten the bends. This condition occurs if a diver stays down too long or surfaces too fast. The extra nitrogen in their blood forms gas bubbles, much like the carbon dioxide in a bottle of soda when it is opened.

The gas bubbles gather in the victim's joints causing excruciating pain. Thus, the name "bends" as the victim bends over in agony. While in the chamber, the pressure is increased to force the nitrogen gas back into a liquid state. Then the pressure is progressively decreased, as if the person is slowly coming to the surface. This gives the nitrogen a chance to be eliminated from the body gradually.

Walking on the beach was definitely something I needed to practice. The unevenness of the sand was a major challenge to someone who couldn't balance that well on flat ground. I staggered along, with my mom holding on to me.

People stared at this young man who looked so drunk in the middle of the day. We let them have their doubts, never stopping to explain. The more I did it, the more proficient I became. Now I walk miles on the beach, and nobody stares (only the cute girls in bikinis).

While taking the treatments, my mom and I stayed in a motel close to the beach. At night, after going out for a sumptuous meal, we would frequent the local pool hall. Each night, my game improved. My hand-eye coordination was coming back.

In the summer, when we returned to New Jersey, I joined my brother Mark in pool games. We would beat our opponents most of the time. That way we got to play for hours. The rule was that as long as you were winning, you could stay on the table. The challenging opponents had to pay for your game.

Chapter 22

It has been said that the sport of golf is like being able to control your life and letting go at the same time. What I believe this analogy means is that on a daily basis we are required to perform extremely well, whether in a career or life in general. This sport allows a person to make a mistake; it does make a difference, but not a devastating one.

Playing golf also took me away from the day-to-day grind of running several successful businesses and providing for my family. I could focus on my game without the constant interruptions of salesmen, phones ringing, people walking in the store, and all other distractions that come with a day-to-day job.

Unable to play for over four years after the AVM, it is hard to describe the great feeling of being able to golf again, especially after my doctor told me it would never happen. Since my balance was gone, when I first attempted to hit a golf ball, someone had to hang on to me from behind so I wouldn't fall over. Because I couldn't follow through with my swing, there was no danger of them getting hit in the head with the club.

With large amounts of practice and dedication, I am learning to hit the ball farther and hope to play and score well again. Now, instead of striving for the ultimate low score, I can relax, enjoy the hole, and be happy just to finish. When at my peak, my golf swing was so well grooved it virtually became automatic. I didn't even have to think about hitting the ball.

On the course, you have only one chance to strike each ball, not like on the practice range where you can continue to hit until it is right. Because I no longer have an automatic golf swing, I prefer to go to the range for practice. I haven't played in tournaments for a few years, and it is a great relief not to have the pressure of people expecting me to shoot a low score.

Golf has proved to be a fabulous way to improve not only my balance but my hand-eye coordination. For my thirtieth birthday, my parents had given me a great gift—a PGA golf school session in Palm Beach, Florida. My wife went with me. We had a great time.

Since I was a fairly good golfer going in, I wondered what they could possibly teach me. Boy, was I surprised to find out how much I didn't know. The teachers were top notch, imparting many new techniques. Integrating them into my game and many hours of practice lowered my handicap.

While at the top of my form, the Rumson Country Club golf pro would recruit me to represent our club in the longest-running intraclub tournament in history—the Quadrangular. We played against the Tuxedo Club in New York and the Morris County and Somerset Hills clubs in New Jersey. One of the most nerve-wracking and difficult aspects of these games was knowing that my fellow club members counted on me to win points against the other clubs' best players.

Being asked to play on the team in many events was a great honor. It was very rewarding to know that my hard work and many hours of practice had paid off, and people were proud of me. I tried to remember an inspiring quote I had heard: "A winner sees a green near every sand trap; a loser sees two or three sand traps near every green." I always strived to be the optimist by only focusing on the green.

I believe that one of the reasons the United States has some trouble doing well in the Ryder Cup, an international team event, is that the pressure to perform well for your teammates is much harder than when you are only playing for yourself. The team relies on you to play your best, and it is embarrassing to let them down.

In football, a good defensive play could be very helpful to secure a win, but in golf this won't work. You can't just go out and tackle your opponent because you're losing—although there were times the thought actually crossed my mind.

*   *   *

My mother's brother sent her an advertisement about the Florida Neurological Institute in Clearwater. Dr. William Hammesfahr, the founder, is a Nobel Prize nominee for his pioneering treatment of neurological problems. These include stroke, brain injury, cerebral palsy, attention deficit disorder, and other learning disabilities.

When my mom called, they agreed to see me for possible treatment. Since Clearwater was across the state, a three-hour drive, we decided to stay in a hotel in the area for our two-week session.

The first order of business was to evaluate my condition. The doctor insisted on an up-to-date CAT scan. Several physical tests revealed, among other deficits, that I had no balance control when my eyes were closed. I was keeping my balance visually rather than with my brain.

The doctor told me to stand with my feet together, a difficult task alone as I always stood with my feet far apart in order to maintain what little balance I had. Then he told me to close my eyes. As he stood close to catch me, I fell sideways. This was proof to him that the balance mechanism in my brain was not functioning properly.

Because an AVM is a weakness in the blood vessels, and the CAT scan revealed that there was some residual malformation left, Doctor Hammesfahr told us that he couldn't treat me with the heavy-duty vasodilators he would normally use. The idea of these medications is to open up the damaged vessels and promote the flow of blood once again.

After two weeks of mild treatments and further testing, he sent us home to continue with a program of injections of magnesium. I also had to drink some foul-tasting concoction. It reminded me of mud. It wouldn't have been so bad if I could have added a shot of Vodka, but on the doctor's recommendation, I had given up alcohol because of my condition.

My mom had to learn how to give me the injections twice a week. We checked my blood pressure each time. If it was too low, I did not get the injection. It was never too low. She had to give me two at once. Sometimes they really hurt, but I never said anything because I didn't want her to feel bad. We kept this up for three months.

Part of my treatment included no more alcohol. The one thing I don't miss is having a hangover the next morning. Anyhow, the way I walked, I felt drunk all the time. Another restriction—no more caffeine—meant no more coffee, soda, or chocolate.

I think I miss the soda most of all. The wake-up jolt of coffee and the sustained high of soda had always kept me motivated throughout the workday. I have learned to live without them.

Before I left Clearwater, Doctor Hammesfahr encouraged me to try to help other brain injury victims. He told me, "I can talk to these people, but you have been through it. When you talk to them it will be important because they will know that you have lived through the situation." These words inspired me to want to help others. If writing this book helps just one person, my life will have had a purpose.

Chapter 23

Every year, my golfing buddies and I planned an adventure to several outstanding courses around the country. We would go for a long weekend, kiss our families good-bye, and spend four glorious days doing what we loved. Myrtle Beach, South Carolina, stands out in my mind as one of the best. With consistently good weather, the courses were always in great shape. We usually played one course in the morning and another in the afternoon. Of course, the nightlife was better in some places than others.

Every time we went to Myrtle Beach, we would relax after our day on the links and have a cocktail. There was an electronic blackjack game in the bar. My friend, Rick, always said, "The drinks are on me!" He would put money in the game and each time would win enough to pay for the drinks. He won every time he played!

We would take our cocktails up to the Jacuzzi, soak up the good feelings, discuss some of our exploits that day on the course, and decide where to go for dinner. One night, gluttons that we were, we played miniature golf.

One day, because Rick was being very mischievous, I started calling him Spanky, after one of the members of the Little Rascals. Somehow, the name got turned around and everyone started calling me Spanky. To this day, the name has held with all my golfing buddies.

Another night, one of my friends, who shall remain nameless, was so drunk that he couldn't even push the buttons on the blackjack machine. Another guy pushed the buttons for him. Unfortunately, he lost all the money that he had accumulated—it had grown to a thousand dollars!

Eventually, as we told our friends at the Rumson Country Club about the great times, our group grew to sixteen. Our wagering system became part of the fun and challenge of the game. The importance was not in the money you might gain. The bragging rights of winning the bets were infinitely more valuable. The betting always consisted of a winner on the front nine, one on the back nine and an overall score. We used our handicaps so everyone would have an equal chance.

There was added money for "snarlies" (when you chip out of the rough by the green and make the putt); "sandies" (when you chip out of the sand trap and then make the putt); "birdies" (when you have one below par); and "greenies" (on par threes, whoever is on the green closest to the hole and sinks the putt in two or less).

One of the expensive aspects of golf is the equipment you need to buy in order to improve. Most people think that the latest golf clubs, the most high tech balls, the newest shoes, will lower their score. Realistically, these items might help, but the best way to get ahead is to practice.

Golf is a mental game as well. There are so many things to remember—stance, hand position, keeping your head down, swing, the take-away, the follow through, shoulder turn, weight shift, and much more. I found that the best thing to do was to zone in on just one thought. Having multiple thoughts as you address the ball creates disaster.

Because of my disability now—not having the best balance—it has become most important that I hold only one thought, rather than the twenty I used to run through my mind, as I hit the ball. I know exactly what I should be doing, but my body doesn't cooperate the way it used to.

In the very beginning of my recovery, we were visiting my sister in Pennsylvania, and she convinced me to try to hit a golf ball. Until then, I had no intention of ever playing golf again. As I stood on the hill, gazing over their cow pasture, I tried to recall all my abilities. My whole family was watching, not thinking that I could do it.

I swung. I missed completely by about two feet. Everyone laughed, including me. Three more hysterical attempts, and I finally connected. The ball flew about 180 yards. We were all elated! This was another baby step on the way toward my recovery.

Through practice, I am advancing every day. It was very disheartening to go from attaining scores below seventy to where I am today. However, the pressure is entirely different. Perhaps I am even enjoying it more. To play just for fun is quite a pleasure.

Since there are many physical changes in my body, my golf swing has undergone important alterations. Originally, I had learned to swing using the upper body muscles. Because my upper body was so strong in the past, I could hit my drive 280 yards on the average. One day, while playing with my brother Mark, I hauled off and rocketed the ball 375 yards. We looked at each other in disbelief. What an overwhelming accomplishment!

Now, my instructor wants me to use my leg muscles more. Swinging this way reduces the torque on my back and will allow me to play comfortably as I grow older. Initially, my yardage with every club (except the putter) was reduced by about fifty yards. I didn't want to hear it, but the pro told me this would happen. Over time, with practice, the yardage will get better. All my friends at the country club have told me they hope I will attain my single digit handicap again soon.

Right now, I play for fun. The stress and pressure are gone. Some people thrive on the stress. In a way, I used to like it too. Earning everybody's respect was enjoyable. Now I earn their respect in a different way—they see how I have overcome adversity.

While I stayed in Florida, my dad would take me to play with his men's group. Although a little frustrating, it was good to get out on the course again. Watching them hit the ball, I would try to connect the way I used to. I wanted to impress everyone. Of course, this did not work. My dad encouraged me to slow down, don't try to hit so hard.

My mom would take me out to play nine holes on a small course, and I could relax and not have to try to keep up with the men. This really helped me hit the ball much better; the pressure was off.

Many friends have asked me to join them on some of my favorite courses. At the moment, I graciously decline since I am unable to play every hole. What a waste of time and money to include me in their game.

It is so hard to sit out on some holes because I don't want to make a "donation" into the hazards that, like lurking monsters, loom up to catch my ball. I certainly would love to play. It just doesn't make sense at this time. I know that eventually this will change.

After playing golf at least four times per week for many years, it was very difficult to accept not being able to play at all. As I am working my way back slowly, perfecting my "new" swing, which is entirely different from my old swing, I am finding more time to get to the golf range.

It is definitely good not to be addicted to the game anymore. Even though I still enjoy it, golf is not the prime focus of my existence. Now I have the time to enjoy some of the things I missed out on.

Having been a good golfer, I have a keen eye for spotting what someone else is doing wrong. Because of this, I have been able to help some of my friends improve their swing and their game.

It's too bad that I could not become a golf instructor. In order to be a professional teacher, you must be able to break eighty, two times in a row. This would be impossible for me now; however, it is something to consider for the future.

Many of my golfing friends have told me how great it was that I was always willing to play with people who did not play as well as I did at the time. My thinking was that when I started, I could barely hit the ball. Practice and playing with more experienced players helped me play better. A lot of low handicappers won't play with those who score higher than they do. I enjoy playing with anyone as long as they are a nice person.

*   *   *

The follow-up to Doctor Hammesfahr's report was to have another CAT scan to study what he had found. Upon my return to New Jersey for the summer, I made an appointment with Doctor Rosenblum.

After another year of therapy, I had become able to maintain my balance with my feet together and my eyes closed for at least a minute, an accomplishment that overjoyed Doctor Rosenblum when I demonstrated it for him. He also had me walk across the room, placing one foot heel to toe with the other. He was totally amazed that I was able to do this.

We gave him the results of my experience with the Florida Neurological Institute. He suggested I see Dr. Alejandro Berenstein in New York City. He would do an angiogram, and if he found a problem, his method of treatment would be to "super glue" (or something like it) on the spot.

As luck would have it, we got an appointment right away and trotted off to Beth Israel Hospital. Doctor Berenstein is the director of the Hyman-Newman Institute for Neurology and Neurosurgery. He is a pioneer in the emerging field of interventional neuroradiology. His method utilizes minimally invasive procedures to treat conditions related to the vascular system of the brain, head, face, spine, and spinal cord.

The doctor reviewed the CAT scan from Florida and agreed that there a problem still existed. He felt that his treatment would correct this. When he tried to fit us in his schedule, he proposed a date in November for the procedure.

Since we were planning to go back to Florida in October, my mom asked if I could be put on the waiting list for an earlier cancellation. He checked in his book and realized that a woman had just cancelled an appointment for the next morning. What serendipity! We spent the night in the city since we needed to be at the hospital at the crack of dawn.

Throughout all my hospitalizations over the past three years, I had never been fully aware of the risks involved with the many procedures that were performed on me. When the doctor gave me the mandatory information that there was a risk of not surviving, I became really upset, realizing for the first time that there was the possibility I would not wake up. My mom reassured me that the doctor knew what he was doing; everything would be fine. I still worried and was overjoyed when it was over.

The procedure was performed like an angiogram. A catheter was inserted in my groin, dye was injected, and as the doctor watched its progress through my brain, he identified the problem area and then inserted the glue-like substance that would close it off. This is a minimally invasive operation, the aftermath only involving getting the site of the entry into my groin to stop bleeding and close up.

After three days in the hospital, Dr. Berenstein sent me home, informing us that he was unable to completely close off the remainder of the malformation. I was a candidate for radio surgery.

There were several hospitals that could perform the radio surgery. Pittsburgh was one possibility, but since my parents wanted to get down South, we opted for the Shands Neurological Center at the University of Florida in Gainesville. Dr. William Friedman uses the LINAC scalpel procedure, a precision radiosurgical instrument that delivers a high dose of radiation to the target area. This carefully placed radiation dose spares the surrounding brain tissue while treating the problem.

I arrived early in the morning at Shands. A CAT scan obtained the exact location of the remaining AVM. A halo, a large metal ring that encircled my head, was screwed into my scalp and forehead with the use of local anesthesia. This ring would prevent any head movement as the procedure was performed.

About ten other patients waited with me, most of them with malignant brain tumors. Once again, after meeting everyone else, I considered myself lucky to have a comparatively minor problem.

The actual radiation treatment only took forty minutes. We spent the day at the hospital as I waited my turn and the doctors continued to check my condition afterward. A follow-up MRI six months later revealed there were no more problems. The LINAC scalpel treatment had been a success.

Chapter 24

Throughout my married life, we had enjoyed lots of great activities. There were many parties, golf outings, ski trips, and vacations. We bought new cars, renovated our house, enjoyed membership in the country club, and went out to dinner often. It was the good life.

Now, I could not afford these luxuries. I had to sell our house and most of its contents. Of course, when my wife had the garage sales, to include my big-screen television, I never saw any of the proceeds. How unfair—I had paid for everything.

Unfortunately, through the horrors of divorce proceedings, my financial credit was ripped to shreds. Before this took place, we had enjoyed pristine credit in every aspect of our lives. After, as my ex-wife's financial obligations were not met on time, our credit standing deteriorated. Over the past few years I have worked hard to successfully restore my good position.

Good health insurance policies that were in place through my business provided the payment for the bulk of my medical bills—they were astronomical. After two years, I became eligible for Medicare. This allowed me to stop paying the monthly premiums for my private insurance, a big help in meeting my financial obligations.

Without a disability insurance policy, my life would have become a total wreck. I never could have survived as well financially on my social security disability alone.

The added monies have enabled me to pursue a lifestyle of relaxation and recovery.

Without the burden of a major financial obligation, I have time to work on regaining my health. There are no regrets about the way I used to live; it was a fabulous lifestyle. But now I have time to do volunteer work, travel, write, and work on my sports and physical abilities. A personal trainer keeps me on the right path with a commitment to improve. That way I don't run off and go to the movies every chance I get.

Travel has become an important part of my life. To see other parts of the world without the obligation to return on schedule gives me the flexibility I never had before. My life is simpler. No more dread of coming home from a relaxing vacation to deal with the daily grind.

On a cruise with my parents to Colombia, South America, I was shocked and saddened to see how some people lived in tiny lean-tos. I never fully realized the extent of poverty in other parts of the world. We take so many things for granted in our great country. Just the fact that most of us have running water and electricity while so many others in the world do not, is a luxury that I have learned to appreciate.

The freedom of choice to go where I wanted, when I wanted, was always very limited. People always depended on me to be there for them. Although fewer obligations to others have allowed me to be independent, I still hope to have influence on their lives in a positive way. Inspiration to keep on trying, no matter what the odds, is on the top of my list.

A budget has become a very useful tool. Living on my own, I have learned to allocate my income wisely. The realization of what it takes to live on a fixed amount of money each month has educated me on how to manage my life accordingly. With a major decrease of funds, I have figured out ways to make the most of what is available. It reminds me of my college days when monies were also limited.

My outlook on life is, and always has been, that if you are a nice person, it does not matter how well off you are financially. I try to accept all people for who they are. This way, I have made many friendships. It is my intention for this to continue.

*   *   *

Swimming has been a large factor in renewing my coordination. Everyone was so surprised when, unable to walk on my own, I could walk fairly well in the pool as the water supported my body. When I tried a few swim strokes and actually did it, my whole family was there, cheering and crying, so elated that I could really swim.

It has continued to be an important part of my therapy, only limited by the time I can spend in the treated water. If I stay in too long, the chlorine irritates the scar that I have on my leg from the skin grafts.

A little kid asked me one day, "What's that big scar on your leg?"

I told him, "It's a shark bite." It really looked like one. His eyes got as big as saucers. I teased him for a few minutes and then finally told him the truth.

After five years of dealing with the ugly scar, I discovered an ointment called Scar Zone. Three weeks of use made the scar nearly invisible; almost like my old skin. I encouraged my dad to try it on his wounds from a triple bypass operation. It worked for him too.

After a year in a wheelchair, as I relearned to walk, exhaustion became a factor. Trying so hard to improve, I was worn out by my efforts. In the beginning, I could only walk about one minute on my own. This extended as my coordination improved, and after three years of practice, I could walk around Disney World only stopping every ten minutes to rest. Now, I can walk for hours.

Physical conditioning has always been an interest of mine. Many people do not have the drive or ambition to go to the gym. I have always found it motivating and enjoyable. In high school, in order for me to have a chance against the larger football players, weight lifting, to build my muscles, became important.

I was small in stature at the time, so being strong was a needed advantage. Now, when I work out, I concentrate more on the leg muscles. They are required on a daily basis for walking. It is a great feeling to prove the doctors wrong when they said I would never walk again on my own.

There are many advantages of good physical conditioning. From helping you move through the day without effort to fighting illness, being in good shape is an important attribute for a high quality of life. Every morning before I get out of bed, my routine is to do two hundred crunches to get my blood flowing. It is best to workout in the morning. The stress that we face on a daily basis will be easier to handle.

Chapter 25

Personal trainers are not for everyone, but I have found their expertise in my situation to be of the utmost importance. Over a five-year period, my various trainers have instructed me in the proper exercises to do, and the correct way of performing them to avoid injury. My physical condition has improved significantly. Before the AVM, I was in very good shape—a major factor that contributed to my survival.

Since I enjoy working out, physical therapy does not feel like a punishment either. In beautiful weather, I could do all kinds of fun things such as go to the beach, the golf course, or the park; instead I opt to go to the gym.

A session with my personal trainer once a week, two more days at the gym on my own, and some type of physical activity on the other days has become my normal routine. My sister, Ginger, made up a daily schedule sheet for me. It proved to be very useful as a reminder to include all my necessary activities each day.

Exercise of some type is important, but eating the proper foods requires constant attention. I no longer rely on diets and weight-loss products to maintain a desirable weight. I basically eat what I want, within reason, until satisfied and work out to burn up the calories.

In the past, I always had to watch my intake carefully so as not to put on weight in the wrong places. Even though I used to go to the gym every other day, I started to get a beer belly from drinking alcohol and eating fattening snacks. It was a constant battle that had to be won.

A good night's sleep is of prime importance, especially while trying to recover. I take calcium every night before bedtime. Sometimes I would wake up in the middle of the night and not be able to get back to sleep, my mind racing with all kinds of thoughts. The calcium not only allows me to sleep through the entire night; research shows that it will help the brain heal itself.

Staying in good physical shape and taking vitamins will improve the immune system. As we get older, our bodies find it harder to fight disease. A good blood flow is important to our health. A daily exercise routine will help this happen.

As our bodies age, our blood becomes thicker, that is why older people get so tired. Physical activity thins the blood, enabling us to have more energy. Drinking water is also essential. These are just some of the benefits of exercising. The worst thing to do for your body is to become a "couch gremlin."

The progress I have made in my physical improvement was done all for an unknown result. Would I ever walk properly again? Would I play golf, surf, swim, or skateboard? Why was I working so hard for this unknown? I had to try. Now, I am in better shape than ever with room for continued improvement.

My goal has always been to strive for excellence not only for myself, but to impress my family and friends. I know they will stand by me no matter what the results of my hard work. I am very grateful for their respect and support. Rising from the abyss of despair has been an interesting journey with everyone's help.

Chapter 26

Because I was unable to drive, many different friends would pick me up to go for lunch or dinner. My everyday life had been changed so drastically, and going out with my buddies was a great diversion.

When I visited my sister and her family in Pennsylvania, her husband, Gene, took me out driving for the first time on their large property. Behind the wheel at last, I tasted the joy of freedom. To be in control, once again, of my own destination made me feel fantastic. It would be a while before I could drive on the road, but this gave me a sample of independence.

For two and a half years, even though I still had a motor vehicle license, I had not been allowed to drive, an incredibly frustrating situation for me. Not to be independent anymore, relying on someone else for my transportation, waiting to go on their scheduled time—all became intolerable. As I recouped my health in Florida, I began practicing my driving skills on my parents' golf cart, navigating the streets and parking lots of Nettles Island.

My peripheral vision was always very good, and I discovered that it still was. One day, as my mother drove in a parking lot, I realized she was about to hit the curb. I grabbed the wheel and turned it, narrowly missing her intended target. She was so impressed with my vision and quick reactions that she realized it was time for me to start driving on my own. My dad had taken me to practice in the large parking lots at the mall and was pleased with my progress.

In the summer, when we returned to New Jersey, my brothers accompanied me to parking lots, and monitored how I was driving. Since I still had my driver's license, this was no problem. They realized that my abilities were still intact. My reactions were getting better. I was on the threshold of being able to go out on the road again.

The following winter, my mom took me to the Health South facility in Vero Beach, Florida. They had all the equipment to evaluate potential drivers and their skills. The machines tested my vision and reaction time. They simulated driving situations to see how I would handle them.

A written test was part of the scenario. After an hour, my mom returned to pick me up. I sat very dejected in the waiting room and told her that I had failed and the nurse wanted to talk to her.

Sad and upset, she told me I could practice some more and come back again. The nurse proceeded to sing my praises telling my mom that I had done so much better than most of the people who came there, and I was absolutely ready to drive.

My mom could have strangled me on the spot for kidding her. She let me drive the hour home. We stopped for a celebratory lunch on the way. I have been on the road ever since, and my dad, who runs a driving school called Driving Dynamics, is very impressed with my skill and ability.

The freedom I finally acquired was indescribable. To be able to come and go as I pleased, not relying on anyone else's schedule, opened up a whole new world for me. I was on my way to total independence. It was the same feeling I had when I first got my driver's license at age seventeen. What fun to feel like a teenager again!

After two years of living with my parents, although it was wonderful, I was ready to live on my own. I did not want to be a burden to anyone any more. Renting a cottage in Monmouth Beach, New Jersey, right around the corner from my brother, Billy, brought me one step further in my quest for independence. With a new car and a place to live, my life was looking up.

Unfortunately, my ex-wife restricted how far I was allowed to drive my kids. She said that they could not go with me for more than a forty-five-minute drive. This seriously hampered what activities I could do with them.

One of the few "perks" of my condition is the handicap card for parking my car. Going to the food store, the mall, the movies, I can always find a spot at the front door. When I took my nephew Will to a football game at Giant's Stadium, the parking lot was packed. As I drove to the handicap area, right near the front gate, he was most impressed. We were being treated like royalty.

The parking spaces for the handicapped are always much wider than normal. This makes me very happy as I hate to get door dings on my car.

Chapter 27

One of the many things I have found time to do is to help others. It is a great feeling to make donations. These can take many forms. For instance, my speech therapist told me about an older man who had a stroke and was ready to quit trying to recover. He had been a golfer who scored in the 80s. So I decided to take him with me once a week to the golf range. As he couldn't drive a car, I picked him up each Sunday. He hadn't hit a ball in many years.

As we began with putting, he was ecstatic when he realized he could actually stroke the ball and get it in the cup. I gave him some tips I had used throughout my golf career. He listened well, and his putting reflected this as he improved week by week.

From there, we moved on to the range. We started out with irons only. They were easier for him to hit than the woods. Each week we noticed an improvement. This was thanks enough for me. I was happy that I was able to help another human being improve his quality of life.

Donating your time is important. To help others in any small way is gratifying. Giving money each week at church makes me feel that I am helping those less fortunate. I give CDs and DVDs to the public library, clothes to the Salvation Army, and half of the proceeds of the sale of this book will go to medical research and various charities.

This world is made up of givers and takers. There are some people who are only takers. I feel best being a giver and have always been that way. Since becoming disabled, I realized the great importance of this trait. On a daily basis, I look to do a favor to help somebody out. Most of them are total strangers; I may never see them again. But maybe they will be inspired to help someone else because of my gesture. In some small way, I am repaying the community for all the help they gave me during my ordeal. This is another way of thanking God.

One day in Florida, while I was trying to cross a busy street to get to the beach, a man I barely knew stopped his car, got out, and halted the traffic so I could proceed. Another time, a man who worked in a convenience store, saw me attempting to cross a major highway. He stopped what he was doing and came outside to help me get across safely. Small kindnesses like this are important. The world just might become a better place for all of us.

My faith has sustained me through my trials and tribulations. Will power and determination have helped me accept the many challenges of my recovery.

Chapter 28

In seventh grade, I bowled on the team with my school. We played in a league. My average was around 170, and lots of trophies came my way. Now, I am ecstatic if I get close to breaking one hundred. My new goal is to break that one hundred mark and continue my fight up the ladder. Frustration put aside, I know that in time I will make it.

One day, at Nettles Island, I decided to try riding a bicycle again. As I hopped on, full of enthusiasm for my potential freedom, I rode ten feet down the street and promptly ran into a parked car. Falling off, I hit my head, skinned my knees, and lost all confidence in any abilities I might have had.

When I tried to ride the bicycle, my hands made the handlebars go back and forth out of control. The damage to my nervous system made me unable to do some things that required the use of my balance. I felt all was lost.

My dad said, "You will ride again. You just need a little practice." He showed me how to get on the bike and glide down the shallow incline of our neighbor's driveway with my legs hanging down for balance. I did this over and over again for days. Finally, I felt that I could balance well enough to try putting my feet on the pedals. More trips up and down the driveway for another week.

The big day came when my dad held the bike steady and ran up and down the street with me. He gave me a push and shouted, "Stop looking down!" I concentrated my gaze toward the end of the street. Once I started looking up, I was able to hold the bike steady and pedaled straight down the street.

As I turned around at the end and rode back, a feeling of triumph filled my heart. I was on the road to freedom! It was amazing what a huge accomplishment this turned out to be. I think it was the end of my depression. It gave me the incentive to try other activities. I realized that I could recover some of the skills I had taken for granted all my life that I thought were lost forever.

Chapter 29

Appreciate what you have. It is so easy to take everything in life for granted. That is human nature. But I had a real wake-up call. One of my favorite quotes is "Life is what happens while you're making other plans." I don't remember who said it, but it is so true.

Every day I come across people looking for angles on how to get rich fast. I worked hard for all the things I have. Money was important, but now my priorities have changed substantially. I am successful by just being alive today. I have gotten a second chance and appreciate the little things in life so much more.

For a long time, when I went to bed at night, I worried about not waking up in the morning. Each morning when I opened my eyes, I was very grateful to see another day.

It is important how I spend my hours. Each hour is precious. When people say to me, "God bless you," my response is, "He already has."

Right now, my priorities are to write this book to inspire others to keep going no matter what the odds, to better my health through exercise and good eating habits, and to be a strong influence in a child's life to help them navigate this complicated world. I was very honored to be asked by my nephew Will, my brother Billy's oldest child, to be his sponsor for his confirmation.

Life is a long road, and it is hard to face it alone. At times, because no one I knew had been through my type of crisis, the feeling of facing the world alone was a big part of my life.

The fact that many people were there to support and stand by me gave me the confidence to continue on the path of recovery. I know I have the devoted support of my family and friends. However, it is entirely up to me to conquer my limitations, build up my capabilities, and enrich my life in general.

Even with this support, sometimes you have to be your own best friend. I thank God every day for the things that make my life better. My philosophy in life has always been, "Be nice to others." This reaps its own rewards. To be friendly and kind to others makes you feel good about yourself. There are many people in this world that need help of some kind. My position is that I can't help all of them, but I will help some of them.

Many people never think about their life here on earth, but we occupy this planet for a very short period. Eternity is forever. I now know that God helped me survive for a purpose. If my story influences just one person to keep going, my goal has been accomplished.

My attitude has allowed me to see the upside of a bad situation. Instead of being upset and sitting at home, miserable about my condition, I look at the possibilities the future holds for me to continue improving. There are many things I want out of life. My pride is what drives me to succeed. The most important person in this world for me to please is myself.

Chapter 30

So much of my early life had been spent by the ocean. I never fully appreciated the beauty and power of nature. Now, a walk on the beach, the wind blowing hard or gently caressing me, the waves crashing or merely lapping the shore, the sea birds diving for fish or running zigzag down the tide line grabbing at morsels—all these beautiful natural events have become an important part of my life.

To see a sunrise or a sunset, to walk through a field of wildflowers, to watch a bird or butterfly take flight are things I never took time to enjoy before. The serenity of the ocean relaxes me. It doesn't care about all my difficulties; it is just there to comfort me. It offers no opinions or suggestions. It gives me strength. Now, I take special moments to appreciate and indulge in the beauty that surrounds each one of us every day. The wonder of life in any shape or form has become a top priority for me now.

Growing up, we went to the Catholic Church. My mom had been educated at the Convent of the Sacred Heart in New York City. She took us to church every Sunday; we attended catechism classes and learned respect for God.

My mother, as a volunteer, taught classes in our basement playroom for many years to prepare kids to receive the sacrament of confirmation. My dad was raised a Presbyterian. At one point, as a young boy, he thought he might become a minister. Instead, he became a racecar driver.

After I got married, church fell by the wayside. I was too busy working, playing golf, going on vacation, or just doing my "honey-do" list. After living through the crisis, I have learned a greater respect for religion. I attend church every Sunday and thank God each morning when I awaken.

The second winter of my recovery, while in Florida with my parents, I decided that in order to thank God properly for all He has given me, I would ask the priest to allow me to address the congregation after Mass. I did this all on my own; my mom didn't know anything about it until that day.

As Mass ended, Father announced that a very special parishioner had something to say. I went to the microphone and told everyone that this was my way of thanking God for all He had done for me.

Even though a lot had been taken away, my life was spared. My feeling was that there is still something here on earth I need to accomplish. There are no guarantees that I will end up in heaven, so by speaking to the congregation, I was thanking God at that time. I hoped to inspire people to think about all they have and be grateful every day of their lives. I got a standing ovation.

Chapter 31

The old cliché "When one door closes, another door opens" seems appropriate in my situation. My lifestyle was exceptional, and even though much has changed, I feel that it is even better. I have met the challenges that were sent my way.

Even with the help and guidance of family and friends, I had to climb the hill on my own. I'm sure there are people who would not have done it, who would have just given up, unwilling to give it the extra try. By perseverance and determination, being willing to go the distance, my lifestyle, once again, is outstanding.

I count myself among the most fortunate of people to be born and live in the United States of America. We have the best country in the world, and we are enjoying wonderful years because of our ancestor's sacrifices to build this great nation.

Today, the young men and women who fight on behalf of our freedom and democracy are making huge differences in our way of life. They should be honored and appreciated for all they have done. I, for one, am thankful.

I never realized how important Memorial Day was, but now value the meaning of the day much more. To remember those who have gone before us—-family, friends, or strangers—to honor their lives in some way, has become important to me.

As many of my friends came to visit me in the hospital, I think they realized the utter fragility of life. Perhaps they would no longer take everything for granted. To see one of their cohorts cut down in the prime of his life must have made them stop and think. I was lucky to survive. One of my friends died of a heart attack several months after he visited me. He was only forty-two.

Having to rebuild one's life is difficult. The knowledge and experience that I accumulated throughout my lifetime have helped me to achieve this goal. Although some things can never be replaced, I have worked very hard on refurbishing all that is possible.

By not giving up, I have made all those people who supported me physically and spiritually very happy, including myself. I will never let them down. My current condition is not what it used to be, but my perseverance will make everyone who has helped me proud of my accomplishments.

I have learned that money isn't everything. Our communities provide so many free activities and events. You don't need to spend a lot of money to have a good time. Now that I am living on my disability income and paying child support each month, I have had to cut way back on spending. My research has found such things as free-rental CDs and DVDs among the books at the public library. Parks provide tennis, basketball, soccer, walking tracks, and open fields for all types of activities. I seldom thought to take advantage of these opportunities in the past.

Chapter 32

Because I grew up in a comparatively small town, I made many lifelong friends. To this day, I have dinner every week with Mike, a pal since fifth grade, my surfing buddy. My friends seem to overlook my deficiencies, not caring that, as one put it, "You are doing great! You just walk like Frankenstein and sound like the Cookie Monster!" I'm just glad he didn't say I look like Big Bird!

Jim, another great buddy, lives in Colorado now. While I was involved with therapy in Florida, he sent a private airplane to pick me up. Staying for a vacation in Boca Grande on the west coast of Florida, he wanted to go tarpon fishing and thought I would enjoy it. The mayor of Telluride, the town in Colorado where Jim lives, accompanied us.

It was a great day of fishing; lots of bites, but no landings. They all got away, but we had the excitement of witnessing these magnificent fish fighting for their lives. The thrill of seeing a six-foot-long creature, silver scales shimmering in the sunlight, leaping clear of the blue water, shaking its head to get free of the lure was unforgettable.

Sadly, Andy, the mayor, died a couple of months later from a heart attack. He was only forty-seven, leaving a wife and child. Jim donates his time as a volunteer fireman in the town, and he heard the emergency call. Andy said, "Jim is here. I'll be fine." They were the best of friends. He died on the way to the hospital. Once again, I realized the great fragility of life.

As timing would have it, I was in Beaver Creek, Colorado, with my parents for the wedding of their good friend's daughter. I had just heard about Andy's death. Jim flew his own plane over to the Vail airport to pick me up so we could attend the funeral together.

It was a cloudy, foggy day, and it took several hours of waiting on the ground for Jim to get a window through the clouds where he could fly in. Somehow the right amount of clearing opened up at the perfect time so he could land. He flew me back the next day in time for the wedding.

During the summer of 2004, I flew to Denver, rented a car, and drove to Telluride. Jim and I had a great time reminiscing about our childhood days of adventure. The owner of a real estate company, he has a pretty wife and two daughters. I respect him immensely as he does very well in his career but still takes the time to volunteer his hours for the fire company. One day, Jim flew us to Las Vegas for the weekend. Another buddy from high school met us there. We had a blast!

Chapter 33

While in the hospital, the entire community was praying for me. Four churches had my name on their prayer lists. People who had never met me before were kind enough to give the support I needed. I am thoroughly convinced that this is one reason I pulled through. The power of prayer cannot be denied. It is wonderful to realize how many good people there are in our world.

In the hospital, I had received myriads of get-well cards. Riverview Hospital had a small chapel by the entrance, and my mother would stop there each morning to beg God to help me. I am eternally grateful for everyone's efforts, and I am living proof that their prayers were answered. I thank God every day.

One of the major lessons I have learned through all my trials and tribulations is that friends are more important than money. Money is nice to have; it makes life a little easier and more enjoyable. But when I am gone, it won't matter how much I had. What will matter is how good and kind a person I was to everyone, family and friends and even strangers. Although money had been my main focus in the past, people are more important to me now. I no longer prioritize my financial position, now focusing my time on building and continuing friendships.

The movie *It's a Wonderful Life* has a great meaning for me. I feel it is exactly the way my friends and family treated me when the chips were down. The community backed up Jimmy Stewart's character when he needed it. That is what the community did for me.

Throughout my recuperation, my whole family constantly researched different avenues to help speed it along. Between the hyperbaric oxygen therapy; the magnesium injections; the speech, occupational, and physical therapies; the spinning theory; the radio surgery; the chiropractic adjustments; and the acupuncture—no stone was left unturned.

When I visited my sister, she took me to a hypnotist, a speech therapist, a masseuse, and a therapist who performed deep myofascia massage. All these methods helped to some extent along the way, but it was my own determination to recover that kept me going.

Some friends have helped me tremendously, not only financially, but with moral support. When I thanked one of them he said, "I know you would have done the same for me if the situation had been reversed." This is so true. I treat all my friends with respect, and they appreciate this. I am thankful beyond measure for their many kindnesses.

Chapter 34

Having always excelled at sports, I became determined to get some of this talent back into my life little by little. Since I am unable to work, I now have the time to devote to this goal.

Science tells us that the left side of our brain controls the right side of our body. My entire life, I was always left-brain dominant; my right side was more coordinated than my left. Now it is just the opposite—a major setback—my left side is more coordinated.

When I stand on the skateboard, I put my left foot on the board with no problem, but getting my right foot on is difficult. Practice with my razor scooter helps because it has a tall handle for support. I know I won't ever be as good as I was in the past, but any small achievement is worth the effort. After being told I would never play sports again, I am happy with my accomplishments so far.

Now, when I walk, I unconsciously hold my right shoulder back. My mom is sure it stems from my days of surfing and skateboarding when I always put my left foot forward, right shoulder back to balance myself. She constantly reminds me, "Relax your right shoulder!" It works for a while, but as soon as I stop thinking about it, back it goes. Subconsciously, I think it helps me balance.

Skiing taught me balance and coordination. This enhanced my participation in all other sports. Since the AVM, I have chosen not to pursue any more time on the slopes. My children loved to ski, and I had just bought new equipment for all of us: skis, boots, poles, and all the clothing that went along for a cold weather sport.

But my decision to stop is based on the fact that I no longer want to subject myself to the cold climate. Skiing was great, and I don't regret leaving it behind. There are many wonderful memories to fall back on. As a final gesture, I donated all my brand new equipment to the Salvation Army.

One of the therapies that helped redevelop my memory was basically playing a game of Concentration. On the computer, I had to turn over one playing card at a time and remember where to find its match.

Another game entailed viewing a picture for thirty seconds, and then fifty words would come on the screen. Approximately twenty were correct for the picture. In the beginning, I could only remember about ten items. After six weeks, I could remember around seventeen. The doctor was happy with my progress.

Chapter 35

As we age, our memories become less efficient than they were in our youth. This, combined with my disability, has had a big effect on my short-term memory. That is why I find it necessary to write everything down.

My memory has improved immensely at this point in time. However, it is still not good enough for me to function properly in the business world. This memory deficit has also prevented me from accomplishing some of my goals as quickly as I anticipated.

Each morning, I number the things I need to do that day. Every day the activities change. I used to visualize the number and the activity together. Each day I would go on a journey, starting at my house, which was number 1. Then, lunch with a friend might be number 4 on my list.

As each objective was completed, I "blew them up" with a "grenade." That is how I knew they had been done and didn't have to think about them anymore. This system really worked for me. It is just another method of dealing with a deficit. Now I just cross the items off the list as they are accomplished.

One of my main difficulties has been remembering small things, like where I put my keys, sunglasses, pens, shoes, everything. This has become torturous in some instances, and now I try to have designated places where I put certain items. This is probably a good method for everyone to follow, especially as they get older.

Writing this book has become an emotional experience for me. On beautiful days, I would rather be outside, hitting golf balls, walking on the beach, and just enjoying life. But as I have said before, if by reading about how I conquered my difficulties will help just one person, it will all be worth my efforts.

Emotionally, my problems have been very difficult to deal with. But everyone says that my sense of humor has pulled me through. I think they are right. At one point, while I was still in the wheelchair, the doctor had prescribed Zoloft to conquer my depression. The instructions said it might cause drowsiness, so my wife gave it to me at night.

For months, I was unable to sleep. Eventually, we discovered that it also warned it might cause excitability. I guess I was the excitable one. When I went to live with my parents, they weaned me off the Zoloft. I have been sleeping like a log ever since.

Now I find it hard to deal emotionally with small aggravations. Before, I would basically ignore most unimportant irritants to my day. Because of my brain injury, it has become difficult to accept some of the disappointments in my everyday life. For instance, I get extremely hurt when my kids don't call, especially if they have said they will. I know they have their own lives to lead, and I try to be understanding and not intrude, but it is so hard for me to deal with this annoying disappointment. It is something I have to work on conquering.

I think as time goes on, I will learn how to control my anger. A doctor has told me, and I now know, that this is an emotional consequence of my brain injury. I try to remember one of General Colin Powell's rules for some thoughts to live by: "Get mad, then get over it."

Chapter 36

If you have too many rules for others to meet, you run the risk of major disappointments. Therefore, the best thing to do is cut back on the rules. This reduces the possibility that your expectations will not be met. My attitude toward others has changed. I accept them the way they are and realize people are not robots that will do everything the way I think they should.

I also have difficulty making decisions. Writing down the pros and cons of a situation enables me to make a more intelligent choice. This has become a very helpful procedure, one that I don't always agree with, but one I can live with. It has been hard to curb my anger at times and not get upset over small incidents.

I know I have to be there for my children and will always be there for them. I saw a pillow that had a saying on it: "A hundred years from now it will not matter what my bank account was, the type of house I lived in, or the kind of car I drove . . . but the world may be different because I was important in the life of a child." I hope to be able to accomplish this by helping my children in any way possible. They have been through a great deal of trauma. In school, they are all maintaining high grades. Perhaps they have thrown their attention into their schoolwork as a diversion from this nightmare.

Every day, I feel like I am on a roller coaster ride, there are so many ups and downs. I'm sure my family feels they are right in the car behind me. Hopefully, they are wearing their seat belts and crash helmets!

Chapter 37

Whenever I see someone helping a handicapped person, I admire them for their efforts. Now that I am on the other side, I realize what devotion these caregivers have.

When I went to therapy in Florida, there was a woman who had been in an automobile accident. She was in a wheelchair. Her husband had to take care of her and their three children. He was completely devoted to her care and the needs of the children. I had great respect for his efforts.

Many days when I amble through the mall, practicing my walking skills, I see groups of handicapped people being pushed in their wheelchairs by their aides. I think highly of these helpers, but I also admire the fact that the disabled people still have a life, they appear in public, they enjoy their surroundings. It is so important to experience life and not sit under a rock. The first year I spent in a wheelchair and didn't go out at all. I was totally bored and felt like a complete loser.

When I saw a blind man hitting golf balls, I realized that he could never enjoy the beautiful scenery of the golf course. In spite of this, he continued to practice, hitting the balls quite well. I was very impressed. This man had overcome an extreme handicap to continue enjoying a great sport. If he could do it, I could do it. I have a high regard for people with disabilities who continuously fight to improve their lifestyles.

There is a book, *The Diving Bell and the Butterfly: A Memoir of Life in Death*, written by a man, Jean-Dominique Bauby, who was totally paralyzed in an automobile accident. Somehow, he was able to get across to his nurse that he wished to communicate.

The nurse was smart enough to realize that he could recognize the alphabet. She made up a chart. As she went through it, pointing, and got to the letter he wanted, he would blink his left eyelid, the only working part of his body. He wrote the entire book this way. My problems seem miniscule in comparison.

A young man who owns a local restaurant spent many years taking care of his wheelchair-bound father, a victim of multiple sclerosis. The roles are reversed as the youth cares for the parent. What an admirable thing for him to be willing to do. Many children depend on their parents to take care of them. They take it for granted most of the time.

The most impressive story of survival comes from the life of Lance Armstrong, the bicycle racer. Despite being extremely ill with cancer, he never gave up hope. His racing career was completely disrupted as he fought for his life. He prevailed and has gone on to win yet another Tour de France, the largest bicycle race in the world. After winning seven years in a row, he has decided to retire.

I can relate to his situation. It is almost exactly what I have lived through. Although Lance is a celebrity, I am just an ordinary person. To me, Lance is a hero. To my friends and family, I am a hero. It does not matter what your celebrity status or your talents might be; everyone is capable of overcoming adversity. You do not have to be a public figure or an important star to prevail over difficulties. With the right attitude, anyone can do it.

Chapter 38

Life is like a ladder that you have to climb. As you progress, you reach different levels. When the ladder was pulled out from under me, relearning everything I used to do became the main focus of my life.

It was as if I were playing a game of Monopoly for thirty-six years, where I had built up my fortunes, and someone came in and flipped the board over. Although it was depressing not to be able to function as I had before, I knew I had to keep practicing, and my skills would eventually come back, although this is still an unknown.

I realized that some people were uncomfortable when speaking to me and assumed they might have a hard time understanding the way I talked. Then I thought maybe they were feeling sorry for me. Somehow, they were not in their comfort zone.

While ordering food in a restaurant, the waitress would always make me repeat my order, not able to understand what I said. This was very frustrating and has made me even more determined to get back to normal. I have gained great compassion and respect for others in similar situations.

I have had to give up some of the beverages I enjoyed before. Coffee, with its jolt of caffeine, is no longer part of my morning routine. I always loved that first cup to get me going. Now, on the advice of my speech therapist, who told me that it adversely effects my larynx and will make me talk worse than I actually do, I no longer indulge. I also don't drink soda with caffeine.

The doctor told me, "No more alcohol." I am heeding his words because I am trying to grow brain cells, not kill them. Actually, I feel drunk all the time since I stagger a little when I walk. This was one of the most difficult abstinences since I always had a great time drinking socially with my friends. But I have learned there are other more important things in life. Good health is one of them.

One night as I had dinner in a seaside restaurant with my family, I excused myself to go out for a short walk on the beach while they all lingered over their drinks. When I came back, the bouncer at the door of the bar said, "Hey, buddy, why don't you do everybody a favor and go home now." He was only doing his job. A friend of mine appeared and explained that I walked like that all the time. He finally let me in. The family had a good laugh about it. So did I.

Another day, while walking in the mall, a security guard approached me thinking I was drunk. I had to show him my driver's license and explain my situation to him. He recognizes me now, nods, and says, "Hello."

After a night of dining with a bunch of my friends, they decided to stay in the bar of the restaurant and play a few games of darts. I stayed to cheer them on. They played for a couple of hours, of course ordering drinks to go along with the game. When it came time to leave, they went out the back door; I went out the front.

As I walked to my car, started it, and drove away, a police car turned around to get behind me and pull me over. He was a local Rumson officer and recognized my name, aware of my condition. I was a great decoy for my friends that night and hoped they appreciated it. When I told them the story, they had a good laugh.

Chapter 39

One of my speech therapists had suggested I take singing lessons. I looked in the phone book for a singing teacher, made a few phone calls, left messages, and nobody ever called me back. I guess when they heard my voice, they must have thought I was totally hopeless. So I went out and bought a karaoke machine. It has been good practice for breath control. I also sing along with the radio in my car (when nobody else is around).

Aikido, a form of karate, also became an important part of my ongoing therapy. It is believed to be one of the most spiritual of the martial arts, developed in the early 1900s. The physical side of aikido involves throwing, joint manipulation, and special weaponry training. It does not focus on striking the opponent although it does teach self-defense.

I wore a karate outfit, a gi, and trained with two long sticks, the *jo*, which represents a staff, and the *bokken*, supposed to be the sword. The emphasis of the art was on the dynamics of movement and the control of one's ki (energy or spirit within the body).

In aikido, there is no ego and no competition. It helped bring an inner and outer balance to my body. The first time I did a somersault on the mat, although it wasn't as good as it used to be, made me realize that I still did have some control over my actions.

Throughout my recovery, there have been many frustrations. One day, in the beginning, when I was still in a wheelchair, my wife was driving me to the hospital for a swallowing test. The car ran out of gas. This was the first time I really felt helpless. I couldn't do anything to alleviate our dilemma. Finally, a Red Bank police officer came along, lifted me out of my car and into his patrol car, and took me to the hospital. He turned out to be a friend I had played football against in high school.

There has been no enjoyment in this situation.

Chapter 40

Several of my friends have told my parents that they are so happy to go out to dinner with me because I have inspired them with my successes. They say my positive attitude lifts their spirits and encourages them to achieve more in their own lives. They marvel at my sense of humor and enjoy being around me. I guess they have conquered any comfort-zone boundaries they might have had.

It is hard for me to tell everyone about my limitations, difficult to explain to all those I meet. But my closest friends understand and accept me the way I am. This makes me very happy. As I explain my condition to them, it helps them relate to me in a better way. They know what I have been through; they know what I have overcome.

Another motivation for me is to come in contact with people who have not seen me in a while. They are so encouraging when they notice and inform me how much improvement they see. My friends and family tell me that everybody is very proud of me. In fact, I am also pleased with what I have accomplished.

A saying that has been very inspirational for me is "There are many people who only dream of success; there are others who wake up every day and work hard at it." Now that I have the time to concentrate on my health and well-being, the opportunity is there to achieve even more great things. This does work to my advantage.

At times, life can be a rat race. There are many obstacles to overcome. Some are much worse than others. As we surmount the hurdles of life, we become smarter and stronger in character. Sometimes I ask myself, "Why did this happen to me?" Perhaps it was because God knew I could handle it. Maybe it was a way of bringing me back to Him. Until then, attending Mass had not been a top priority in my life. I don't know the reason, but I am dealing with it.

I now know that many other people have burdens they must carry. Another interesting quote comes from Plato (c. 427-347 BC): "Be kind, for everyone you meet is fighting a hard battle." It seems nothing has changed very much over the millennia. Helping people in any way possible has become valuable to me. I have met a challenge and hope to inspire others to do the same.

Chapter 41

Give respect to gain respect. Growing up, we tried to follow the Golden Rule: treat people as you would want to be treated. I feel that my life achieved the American Dream: a nice home, decent cars, and good family. I have had all this and more.

Whenever I walk in the mall, I remember how it felt to be in a wheelchair. This surely makes me appreciate the fact that I can walk again. Now I do it as often as possible: in the park, at the gym track, on the beach, around my neighborhood. The best part is that I enjoy walking, and it gives me an incredible sense of freedom. Sometimes it takes a major life-changing event to make one appreciate the little things in life.

While at the gym one day, descending a flight of stairs, I realized that there was a day, long ago, when I took this physical feat for granted, and then there was a day when I couldn't do it at all. I had never dreamed that something so devastating would take over my life. It felt wonderful to have the proficiency to be able to navigate the stairs once again.

One of the interesting moments of my recovery came one night while I was still wheelchair bound. We went to the country club for dinner. It was one of my first outings. When people realized I was there, they rushed over to see me. It ended up with a half-hour long "receiving" line. I should have felt like a celebrity. Instead, I felt overwhelmed. It was too much for me to handle at the time, and I had to leave without greeting everybody.

Chapter 42

No matter how bad your life seems you must think of others who are far worse off. Realizing that life has a limited time frame, I am going to make the most of what is still available. This second chance has been a big bonus. My friends tell me that I am fortunate to have another shot at life. Many of them feel that they could not have overcome the difficulties I experienced and still survive.

It is wonderful to have the support and admiration of others, but the saying "The only person that has to think you are special is you," has a tremendous meaning for me now. To be proud of your own accomplishments brings incredible satisfaction to your life.

One day, as I drove through the shopping mall, a woman ran a stop sign and T-boned my brand new car, a Honda Element. I was so upset but eventually realized it could have been much worse. If I had been one second slower, she would have hit me right in the driver's side door. As it was, the accident bent the rear axle and drive shaft.

The police arrived, gave her a ticket for careless driving, and left. My rear tire was flat so I called AAA for assistance. They came and changed the tire. Not really knowing what to do at that point, I was in shock and thought about driving home since it was only a short distance. Right at that moment, another police officer arrived out of nowhere. How fortunate for me that he looked at my tire, realized there was something radically wrong and said, "Sir, I suggest you do not drive that car."

As luck would have it, when the mechanic put it on the flat bed, the axle broke. What a dangerous situation this would have been in if I had been driving it at the time. The lady who hit me stuck around through all this and gave me a ride home. I had told her she could leave, but she decided to stay. She could easily have left the scene but chose not to abandon me. I would have had no recourse if she had just driven away.

When I told my friend Mike about my escapades, he said, "Brother, you really do have nine lives." Someone is definitely watching over me.

My progression from a wheelchair to where I am today inspires those who know me to continue fighting for what they want to achieve—if I can do it, they can do it. Although it has required many years of therapy and hard work, it was worth the effort. To help other people is not a requirement, but to give something back to society is very fulfilling for me.

I learned many lessons through this unbelievable experience, but the most important is to not give up. Even when others tell you there will be no more progress, be persistent, keep trying, there is always hope. As long as I can take a breath, as long as I can enjoy each day for what it brings, I am happy.

Chapter 43

All the sports and activities that were part of my youth are now very helpful for me as I deal with my current situation. Golf taught me how to handle frustration, lifting weights kept me in good shape and made stress easier to cope with, surfing and skateboarding gave me good balance. Another quote I remember is "The winner always has a program, the loser always has an excuse." How true this is!

The results of my efforts to regain all my lost skills have motivated me to continue my progress. The business knowledge I had acquired throughout my life helped me tremendously.

Always willing to do whatever possible to achieve my goals, there were times when I had to make changes in my thought processes to get the desired results. By writing them down, I have been able to go in the right direction. If something was not working the way it should, my willingness to change became an asset.

A question I continually ask myself is, "What is my expected outcome?" It is much easier to make a decision when you recognize the final goal. I now demand more from myself than anyone would ever imagine. My willingness to "go the extra mile" has given me the taste of triumph that no one, including myself, ever expected me to achieve. It has truly been a miracle!

Surfing is still a dream. After college, I stopped riding the waves mainly because I had some bridgework done in my mouth to take the place of seven teeth that never grew in. It being an expensive treatment, I didn't want to take the chance of getting a mouthful of surfboard and wrecking my new teeth. But the eternal call of the ocean is still there.

Recently, I discovered a new soft surfboard, one that does not deteriorate in salt water. Presently, I practice trying to stand up on it in the pool. Since I no longer need to catch the largest waves possible, I am having a great time riding on my stomach, using it like an overgrown boogie board.

At this time, it is impossible to stand up on the board, my hands and arms shake so badly as I try to raise myself. In order to overcome this situation, my trainer at the gym has had me place a basketball on the floor and do push-ups on it. The shaking has somewhat subsided. With continued practice and determination, I will conquer the waves once more.

My son Keith loves skateboarding. Determined to get back some of my expertise in this field, I spent several hours each day honing my skills. At first, I held on to a wall and kept trying to let go. Slowly, with lots of practice, I began to roll down a hill on the board, keeping my balance. I know that most forty-one-year-olds can't even stand on a skateboard, but I remembered how I performed in the past and wanted to get that feeling back.

On an asphalt tennis court, I tried to balance on my board, pull myself along the net, and then let go. To my surprise, the board rolled out from under me, my balance failed, I fell on my head, splitting it open, and sprained my finger trying to break the fall. Bruised and bleeding, I skulked home to lick my wounds. What a blow to my ego!

Most people would have been finished at this point, but the next day, after much persistence, I let go of the net, pushed off, and rolled across the court on my own.

What an incredible reward for all my hard work! This accomplishment was gratifying and monumental.

I realize that we can't always control what problems befall us, but we can control the resolution. In the beginning, it would have been nice if I could have wished my troubles away. However, prayer and hard work proved to be the only answer. My life has been blessed way more than I ever could have imagined. If life is a quest for a treasure, my treasure is that I am here. This path definitely works for me.

(left to right)
Keith Lisa, Jr. Keith, Jr. Amanda
2003

Chapter 44

My life was taken over by the *d*'s. *Disaster* struck in the form of the AVM. *Devastation* came as I lost everything I had worked so hard for. *Divorce* attacked me as the person I had loved more than anything in the world decided to bail out. *Disruption* of my fabulous lifestyle was hard to take.

As my life crumbled, *depression* set in as a result of everything that was happening to me. *Disappointment* at not being able to see my family every day became a deep hurt. A part of my life had been *destroyed,* never to be replaced.

To *dwell* on the past will not help my future. It became very *disempowering* as I lost control of almost everything and everyone I dealt with. People I worked with used to listen to my suggestions and ideas. As they became unwilling to take my advice, I felt like it was a great waste of my time and energy. Not knowing what my future held, what the outcome of my hard work would be brought *despair*, a feeling of complete hopelessness.

It seemed that my life *deteriorated* as I watched my friends and associates get ahead financially. This situation was very *degrading* to me. I had to hold on to the belief that in life one is not judged by your financial position, but by the friendships you develop.

Only a few people had kicked me when I was down. My true friends never took advantage of my helplessness. They lifted me up physically, emotionally, and spiritually. However, I was *disheartened* by those who let me down; those individuals I had trusted. Someday these hurts will heal.

There was *distraction* from my original plans for life as I was set on another path, a path I never would have chosen, but one that I faced and learned to accept.

Dissatisfaction became an asset as I strived to master the skills and abilities needed to recover. My therapists found it hard to understand why I was such a perfectionist. They felt I should be happy to get by with the least amount of effort. That was not good enough. I'm sure I am where I am today because I was willing to put in the extra work necessary for enduring and conquering adversity.

My *diligence* and *dedication* paid off. No one forced requirements on me, but I realized it was up to me to act. I was the only person who could bring my life back into a semblance of order. At first, it was hard to accept being told what to do all the time. I treated these orders as suggestions. It was my choice to act or not.

At times it was very hard, but the final outcome has been worth the journey. Even though I still "walk like Frankenstein and talk like the Cookie Monster," my progress is beyond belief. It would have been very different if I had given up hope.

The lifesaving *d* became *determination*. I was one of the 10 percent to survive a life-altering AVM. God had given me a second chance. I was determined to give it my all and make the best of very difficult circumstances. A person does not know their true capabilities until confronted with a unique situation.

My *drive* and self-motivation had always been good, but this was a major test. It gave me the feeling that I had traveled into myself and discovered the essence of who I truly am. In a way, I had failed my family, although not on purpose.

Realizing that everyone is not perfect has become a great asset in my interactions with other people. Knowing that everyone has some type of burden to bear, we must all have the strength to do what is necessary to get ahead.

Life has actually become *delightful*. With much less stress, much more time to do the activities, I have learned to enjoy and to help others.

It is good to be alive. I know that there are people out there who will benefit from reading my story. Even though I was facing the world of recovery on my own, there were so many people who were incredibly supportive. There were times when I felt like quitting. This would have let down not only myself but also those who were good enough to stand by me through thick and thin.

Each day brings you a choice. You can choose to be positive or be negative. You can sit in the house feeling sorry for yourself or meet each day with renewed vigor and inspiration to get better. Whether it's a major hurdle you are trying to conquer or just an ordinary day, it is best to meet the challenge with the determination to make the most of the time you have been blessed with.

You can be a victim or a survivor. I choose every day to be a survivor. What is inside me has driven me to succeed. This philosophy applies to everyone's life regardless of what condition they are in. I sincerely hope that others might pick up on this determination to do well no matter what the odds.

Whether you are a victim of cancer, stroke, some other disease or traumatic injury, you and you alone have to decide to fight your way back. Even though the descent into despair and the weight of loss might be great, the fortitude to recover and realize the final results will be worth the fight.

Who I am is not how I walk or talk but who I am inside. Ralph Waldo Emerson wrote, "What lies behind us and what lies before us are tiny matters compared to what lies within us."

I have learned what my capabilities and limitations are. I recognize the value of hard work. Focusing on the future has helped me to persevere. Wisdom is in knowing the right thing to do; integrity is doing it. Too many people never really try.

I do not know why this challenge was sent to me, but with patience and persistence I will overcome these difficulties. I possess a certain passion for life that might never have emerged and now appreciate the mystery, beauty, and joy life brings.

Somehow we are all tested every day. Dealing with adversity has made me a better person. Some can't believe that I am not angry over this entire situation. The whirlpool of despair tried to suck me down, but I fought my way back.

My outlook is that it has been a monumental test of my integrity. Perhaps it is God's plan. You may ask if I will ever give up. I answer, "Never!"

Printed in the United States
124712LV00005B/34-36/P